THE LIVING THOUGHTS LIBRARY
Edited by Alfred O. Mendel

[18]

SAINT PAUL

MAP SHOWING THE VOYAGES AND TRAVELS OF ST. PAUL

THE LIVING THOUGHTS OF

SAINT PAUL

PRESENTED BY

JACQUES MARITAIN

[3rd ed.]

CASSELL

AND COMPANY, LIMITED
LONDON, TORONTO, MELBOURNE
AND SYDNEY

[1948]

SAINT PAUL

" SAUL who is also Paul "—" a Hebrew of Hebrews," was born at Tarsus in Cilicia during the Dispersion ; his father enjoyed Roman citizenship.

Brought up in the strictest Judaism, a pupil of the great Pharisee doctor Gamaliel, he first persecuted the infant Church and sanctioned the murder of Stephen. Following his conversion on the road to Damascus, he lived only to preach Christ and to suffer with Him. " Woe to me if I preach not." His apostolic journeys are related in the Acts of the Apostles. His epistles to the Christian communities and to his companions in the apostolate were probably written during the last seventeen years of a ministry which lasted for thirty years. They form both the most burning testimony of evangelical love and the most valuable treasury of Christian doctrine. From this treasury all the Fathers and Doctors—especially Saint John Chrysostom, Saint Augustine and Saint Thomas Aquinas—drew their inspiration ; from it Christian thought has always drawn and never will cease to draw nourishment.

Twice imprisoned in Rome, the Apostle of the Gentiles was put to death under Nero probably in the year 67.

Translation by Harry Lorin Binsse

FIRST EDITION, NOVEMBER 1942
SECOND EDITION, JANUARY 1945
THIRD EDITION, FEBRUARY 1948

PRINTED IN GREAT BRITAIN BY
MORRISON AND GIBB LTD., LONDON AND EDINBURGH

TO

RUTH NANDA ANSHEN

WITH RESPECT AND FRIENDSHIP

is dedicated
this commentary
on the Great Doctor of Grace and Freedom
a Hebrew of Hebrews
the Apostle of the Gentiles

Both author and publisher wish to express their gratitude to the Editors of the Westminster Version of the Sacred Scriptures for generous permission to use their new translation of the Scriptures from the original Greek and Hebrew texts. Extensive quotations have been made from the Acts of the Apostles and from the Epistles of Saint Paul.

SAINT PAUL

INTRODUCTION

"SALVATION IS FROM THE JEWS."[1] IT IS FROM ISRAEL THAT came forth the Saviour of the world ; it is in the womb of a young Jewish girl—the only absolutely pure creature among all purely human creatures—that the Word through Whom all has been made took on human flesh— only to be greeted at once with the first pogrom of the Christian era, the massacre of the little Jewish innocents among whom King Herod sought gropingly to strike down their King ; and no sooner was He born than He was carried off along the highways by Joseph and Mary. Who are these but an indigent family of minor artisans, penniless, without papers, without visas, the first Jewish refugees of the Christian era, with their poor, tired donkey. (Whenever in the history of the world the second Person of the Trinity is sent, He has always to begin by hiding amongst those who cannot recognize Him.)

It is from Israel that came forth the Saviour of the world. The Apostles were Jews. The two greatest leaders of souls that the history of humanity has ever known—Moses and Paul— were Jews. Both of them spoke with God. Both were men troubled by infirmity, were weak and trembled at their terrible mission. Moses was slow of speech, Paul was " buffeted " by an illness which humiliated him. They both appear to us as stamped with an awful majesty ; but they were both vaga-bonds along the roadsides. And Moses was meek, above all men,[2] and Paul supported, with a tenderness tearing at his heartstrings, the first faithful of the infant Church as " his little children." The one and the other were persecuted and abandoned. And since Paul was to be of a pattern with Christ, he was stoned, imprisoned, martyred. Moses transmitted to Israel the tables of the Law ; Paul, by the sword of the Word which was entrusted to him, taught the universal Church,

[1] John iv. 22.   [2] Num. xii. 3.

I

" the Church made of Jews and of Gentiles," spiritual Israel, that it was, " through the Law," " dead to the Law," in order that it might live to God.

*　　*　　*

That is the essence of Paul's mission. That is its central importance in human history. It is through him, and owing to the inspiration he received to this effect, that Christianity became conscious of its liberty from Judaism, of its pure universality. There was a capital event, the greatest in all the history of souls and of civilization. It was necessary to understand that the Son of Man had come not only for the Jew, but for Man, for the human race in its whole unity. It was necessary to understand that the Messiah of the Jewish people had come not only for the Jewish people, but for all the nations of the earth. It was necessary to understand that in saving by his blood men of all the nations of the world, he did not ask them to make themselves Jews, or Judaizers, in order to become Christians, but on the contrary made of them *his own* true Israelites, in spirit and in truth, his people, circumcised at heart, not in the flesh, to which those who came out of circumcision and those who came out of non-circumcision were equally called to belong. It was necessary to understand that the Church, or the Kingdom of God journeying here below, the Kingdom of redemption carried on from generation to generation, was neither a Jewish sect nor a religious extension of the theocracy of Israel over all the peoples of the earth, but rather a universal body newly brought to life in its visible reality by the invisible power of the blood of Christ and the Spirit of God, and all that precisely at the cost of the earthly Kingdom of which Israel was thenceforth deprived. It was necessary to understand that this extraordinary break—whereby from out of the Temple, broken, dispossessed, falling in ruins to the earth, was to arise and become separate the spiritual Israel, the mystical Temple of the body of Christ—was itself conditioned by the straying of Israel and the great misfeasance of its priests. It was necessary to understand that if salvation is for all men and if in Christ there is neither Jew nor Gentile, it is because the power that works salvation is not the Law of the Jews but faith in Him Who was crucified in the name of this Law.

*   *   *

Hence the great intuition which enflames Paul's mind is the feeling for the universality of the Kingdom of God, and the feeling of salvation by faith, not by Law. Another intuition, inseparably bound to the former, is that of the primacy of the internal over the external, of the spirit over the letter, of the life of grace over exterior observances. This is the very spirit of the Gospel. Paul understood more deeply than anyone else the immense spiritual revolution carried out by Jesus, which Saint Thomas Aquinas illuminates when he shows that because the Old Law was a written law, what mattered most therein was the external fulfilment of rites and prescriptions ; but that the New Law is primarily and before all else an unwritten law—written by God in the hearts of those called to Him— and that what is primary therein, and " that in which consists all its power," is the grace of the Holy Spirit operating in souls by means of faith and charity.[1]

Thenceforth purity of heart matters more than the purifications of the Law, mercy more than the sabbath. The distinction between the sacred and the profane orders is not abolished ; rather is it confirmed ; but religion no longer consists above all in the envelopment of the profane by an external apparatus of the sacred in order to subject the former to the law of a God of fear and in order to protect it against His severity. Thenceforth religion consists above all in the penetration of the profane, as well as of the sacred, by the gift of internal grace which transmits to souls the very life itself of a God of love. The whole field of action and existence of the human person, in the category of the profane as in the category of the sacred, becomes the field of interior sanctification, and the social function of the sacred is to serve as an instrument for this sanctification, this spiritualization.

The letter and all external observance are not suppressed, but from henceforth it is realized that they have value only as ordered toward the spirit and vitalized by it. Doubtless they

[1] *Sum. Theol.* i–ii. 196, 1.

will, by reason of human weakness, keep on struggling against the spirit and wishing to gain the upper hand over the spirit, but the tribulations of the saints and the catastrophes of world history will be the price exacted by the vengeful spirit.

The Law has not been done away with ; not an iota thereof has been erased. But Jesus has realized its fulness and perfectly accomplished the work for which the Law was set up. The ceremonial observances, which were figurative and foretold the mysteries of salvation, have come to reality and been consummated in the body of the Messiah and in His sacrifice, and thus they have come to an end—absorbed into the reality which they foretold and prefigured—so that they gave way to the rites and sacraments of the New Law which transmit and perpetuate that reality. The moral precepts, which related to the effective conduct of each man here on earth as that conduct should terminate in the true last End, have in no sense been abrogated, but their meaning has been profoundly changed. The illusion whereby it was believed that man could, by fulfilling these precepts, constitute himself by himself in a state of justice, natural or legal—that illusion has evaporated. It is by the free gift of Himself which God makes us, and by the cross of Christ and by His blood that man is constituted into a state of justice through grace—ransomed at a great price and without having deserved it. Bound to fulfil, and unable by himself to fulfil, these moral precepts in their integrity, in view of a so-called wisdom and perfection which he might owe to his own power as a man, he is bound to fulfil them, and can fulfil them in their integrity—in view of a true wisdom and perfection which he will owe to the power of God—through grace which, if only a man does not refuse it, makes of him a new creature, so that what he has heretofore done or not done has no common measure with his reception of such a gift.

We shall all be judged by our works ; and the works of the New Law are in themselves more difficult than those of the Old Law, in the sense that the former requires the purity of the internal act and of the hidden movement of the soul. But it is not our works which save us. It is Christ crucified and the living faith received from the Father through Him, which incorporates us in Him—the faith which, operating through charity, makes fruitful the works which are prescribed, makes them meritorious, and makes easy of accomplishment that which in itself would be more difficult. So it happens that love is the fulness of the Law, and that we are saved by faith, not without works, but with charity and the works of charity. (With charity whence proceeds works, and without which works are nothing. With the works of charity which, being the active and living completion of our liberty suffused with grace, are the very workings in us of the grace which has been given us.) That man should thus always be held to the works of the Decalogue and that he is, nevertheless, saved by faith ; that he should be freed by faith from the regimen of the Law whose moral prescriptions he is nevertheless required to fulfil —that is the central problem which Paul had here to solve, and which, in the course of centuries, has put great religious thinkers to the test. Many of them have stumbled over the problem because in this or that they parted company with Paul. Here is not only a problem to be solved by a correct arrangement of concepts ; it is also a mystery to be penetrated even more deeply by the intelligence of contemplation.

* * *

The third intuition that illuminates all Paul's thought is the intuition of the freedom of the sons of God. Saint Paul is the greatest Doctor of freedom ; the feeling for freedom is rooted to the very marrow of his bones, in him who was Saul, the most fervent of the Pharisees—whose heart was melted, and all barriers broken by the vision of Christ in glory. From thenceforth he has no boundaries, he is at the service of Him Whom he loves, and Who has set him free. Who will separate him from the charity of Christ ? He lives, and it is not he, it is Christ Who lives in him. He is weak, he is perpetually in anguish—yet he can do all things in Him Who gives him strength, he knows that all things work together for the good of those who love God, he knows that in love and through love the creature becomes one spirit with God.

He knows that freedom, in which we are established by faith, is only achieved and fulfilled—thanks to the Cross—by the Spirit and by love. To say that " charity is the bond of perfection " is to say that it is the soul of freedom. A freedom without charity is a corpse of freedom ; it disintegrates in the misery of created things ; it rots away. The law, which is a tutor, educates us for freedom. As we follow the narrow paths of the moral law, so long as it is the love and the Spirit of God which keeps us to them, we little by little learn to be free : free of evil and sin—and at last free of the law itself, since then we fulfil the precepts not through fear but through love, and as though willing them of ourselves and from what is deepest in us, our will having been transformed into the will of Him we love. The saints are the only truly and fully *auto-nomous* men, for they have lost themselves in their uncreated Principle Who, being subsistent Love itself, is subsistent Free-dom itself, in Whom the law that rules creatures has its seat, and Who is Himself subject to no law. Wherever is the spirit of the Saviour, there is freedom. Those who are led by the Spirit are no longer *under* the law. Nor are they above the law. They have passed on into the other side of things, they are in the inner substance of the law, where the law is no longer seen from without as law, but from within, as love. From thence they look upon the order the law imposes on things as the shadow of love thereon.

> *God is love, it is His shadow*
> *Which is the order of the Law.*[1]

Of themselves they abound in all goodness, forgetfulness of self, wisdom and holiness. " Against a man who is of such sort there is no law."

Thus mortifying his body and following the road, Paul ended up where there ceases to be a road, where there is only the eternal rejoicing of Christ with His poor. He was carried up to the third heaven, but only to bear the stigmata of the Lord Jesus and to fulfil in himself what is lacking in Christ's passion, he furnishing to Him, as it were—here is the law for all the living members of the mystical body, and pre-eminently for the saints—a surplus human nature to suffer here below and to ransom time, day after day. Overflowing with the gifts of

[1] " Dieu est amour, et c'est son ombre
Que l'ordre de la Loi."
Raïssa Maritain, *Lettre de Nuit*, Paris, 1939.

the Spirit, the graces of mystical contemplation and prophetic power, he is the master of masters for Christian perfection and union with God. It is to him above all others that would be attached a Saint John of the Cross. The irresistible dynamism which runs through all his teaching draws souls toward that perfection of charity which, as Saint Thomas Aquinas would explain, is not merely counselled, but commanded, and which comes under the first commandment of the New Law, not doubtless as something to be instantly realized (that is quite impossible), but as the end to which we are summoned and at which all Christian life should aim. Endlessly working to effect the death of the old man, who, in a soul living by grace, is already visited by the principle of death, but whose death that soul must ceaselessly accomplish, all ascetic effort aims at the freedom of the perfect, which is not won, but only prepared, by the work of man, and which is received from the life of God descending into us. Rooted and founded in charity, born of faith and incorporated in Jesus Christ, the new man thirsts to see Him Whom he loves ; and it is love which, across the enigmas wherein divine things appear to us as in a mirror, gives faith a deepening experience of wisdom, and, carrying us on from clearness to clearness, brings us at last into the shining cloud where we possess without seeing it the substance of things hoped for, and understand with the saints what is breadth and length and height and depth, and know the charity of Christ, above all knowing, so that at last the fulness of God may come to fill us to overflowing.

*   *   *

In the chapters that follow there will be found grouped together the principal texts wherein are expounded these Pauline themes. There also will be found the texts relating to the more significant of the other elements in Saint Paul's teaching, where the natural fire of an inspiration more profound than all the developments that theology can draw therefrom illumines the whole of Christian dogma and Christian morals, and especially Christology.

But Saint Paul's teaching is inseparable from his experience. He was not simply called, as were the other Apostles ; he was

converted ; he was the first great convert chosen to carry afar
the name of Christ, and his teaching mission is the extraordinary
flowering of that even more extraordinary moment—his
interior conversion. It is therefore supremely important for
us to know something about his experience, to the extent that
he himself bears witness to it, and to know something of his
life and his apostolic journeys. For this reason it seems well
to begin with the succession of events related in the *Acts of the
Apostles*, and with the text in which Paul himself tells us of his
life and his vocation.

THE EPISTLES OF SAINT PAUL

The Epistles of Saint Paul, arranged in what seems to be the best established chronological order, are as follows :

> First and Second Epistles to the Thessalonians
> First and Second Epistles to the Corinthians
> Epistle to the Galatians
> Epistle to the Romans
> Epistle to the Ephesians
> Epistle to the Colossians
> Epistle to Philemon
> Epistle to the Philippians
> Epistle to the Hebrews
> First Epistle to Timothy
> Epistle to Titus
> Second Epistle to Timothy.

All these were written in Greek.

Jacques Maritain has selected the essence of Saint Paul's thought from the *Acts of the Apostles* (written by Luke) and from the Epistles. The texts selected from the Epistles have been grouped together according to the principal matters dealt with, which it is hoped will make easier the reading of these extracts. In every case a reference is given to the source of what is quoted.

For the Epistles as for the Acts, use has been made of the Westminster Version of the Sacred Scriptures, but original translations have been used when occasionally it seemed preferable.

Chapter I

THE LIFE OF SAINT PAUL

" A Hebrew of Hebrews "

SAUL WAS BORN OF A FAMILY OF PURE JEWISH LINEAGE AT Tarsus in Cilicia. His father enjoyed the privileges of Roman citizenship. Saul was born a Roman citizen. Conformably to the practice of many Jews of the diaspora, he was given two names, one Hebrew—Saul—the other Latin—Paul. As has been pointed out by Ramsay, if Luke had given him his full Latin name—perhaps Gaius Julius Paulus, to select a name possible and even not improbable—historians would have been spared certain futile considerations concerning him, as, for instance, that he was a narrow, one-sided Jew. After his conversion he was to keep the name Paul, leaving Saul aside —perhaps to emphasize that from thenceforth he was a new man.

Tarsus was at that time one of the most flourishing cities of Asia Minor. Celebrated schools were there in abundance, wherein converged cultural currents from both Orient and Occident. Saul's father was a Pharisee. One may suspect that in his early education Saul acquired little from his Hellenic environment. His Greek was ever to remain a language full of life, vivid, colloquial, excellent in expression and movement, but having nothing to do with the Greek of the schools. Yet he acquired, doubtless more through the channels of Hellenistic or Judaeo-Greek literature than through immediate contact with the Greek teachers of Tarsus, the Hellenic culture suitable to a man of liberal education, and thereof his writing gives some evidence.

At Jerusalem, whither he was sent to finish his education, he was a pupil of those Doctors in whose midst had appeared the child Jesus, older than Saul by a few years. The two schools which at that time shared the students of Jerusalem—both of

Pharisee discipline—were the school of Hillel and that of Schammai. It was the first which claimed Saul. He began his study of sacred science at the feet of Hillel's successor, the Rabbi Gamaliel, the great Doctor of the Pharisees, highly regarded by all the people, who was one day to undertake—at the time of the first apostolic preaching following Pentecost—the defence of the Apostles against the Sadducees.

From this rabbinical education Paul was to preserve an incomparable knowledge of Scripture, and that subtle and refined manner of argument—very different from the Greek syllogism—which follows, among all similes and appropriations of meaning, the intuitive thread of one or another of the multiple meanings of the sacred text, and often makes use of composite quotations and long strings of texts.

It is well known that the Pharisees burned with zeal for the integrity of doctrine and tradition, and for a precise and rigorous observance of the Mosaic Law. Only too often this zeal was a human and a bitter zeal. Blindness of the heart joined to an overbearing ardour for religion and to a subtle intelligence and a hatred of error and to that tireless desire to make oneself morally beyond reproach, just by oneself—that which has remained the most commonly recognized characteristic of Pharisaism—is one of the mysteries of our human weakness, whenever it hardens itself in order to raise itself up. I can imagine Saul at the age of thirty or thirty-five, an ardent and pious little Jew, more strict than anyone else in those holy observances which nevertheless do not root the heart in justice, devoted with all his strength to the science of the sacred writings, and convinced that it was the function of the pure of Israel themselves to administer the interests of God. He has placed himself at the disposal of the religious leaders of Jerusalem ; he is " full of zeal for God " ; he believes that he honours His name by persecuting the new sect which speaks in the name of a blasphemer who called himself the Son of the Most High God, and who was condemned to be crucified by the leaders among the priests and whose disciples now lead the people astray by claiming that he is risen from the dead.

The Martyrdom of Stephen

In Peter's first discourses and in the first evangelical preaching, it appears that the efforts of the Apostles were in the beginning directed—by asking the Jews to repair their fatal mistake, and to acknowledge as the true Christ that Jesus whom they had crucified [Acts ii. 36]—toward establishing a Church which would have been the house of Israel itself converted to its Saviour, and spreading His name among all nations. "For to you is the promise and to your children, and to all 'that are afar, even to as many as the Lord our God shall call to him'" [Acts ii. 39]. "I know that ye did it in ignorance," said Saint Peter to the Jews, "as did also your rulers" [Acts iii. 17]. At the time when Stephen was chosen to serve tables, a great number of Jews who spoke in Aramaic or Greek were becoming converted, and even, at Jerusalem, "a large multitude of the priests" [Acts vi. 7].

But precisely from the occasion of the martyrdom of Stephen the opposition of the princes of the priests to the progress of the Gospel became more and more powerful. It was necessary at all costs to stop short this dangerous movement. Everywhere persecution assailed those who became Christians. In the ancient world formalist Jews were to become the instigators of violence directed against apostolic preaching. It was little by little, and with sadness, that the Apostles, and Paul himself after his conversion, had to admit that without question the house of Israel had not only condemned Jesus, but also thereafter opposed faith in Jesus crucified, and thus fulfilled the mystery of its own exclusion. By a strange circumstance, Saul the persecutor played a part in the process of this exclusion of Israel, by virtue of which, as Paul the converted was later to explain, the nations were to "enter in," and the Church be what it was to be according to God's economy—the spiritual and universal Israel of the New Covenant, freed of the regimen of the Law, free by grace and by faith, made up of Jews and of Gentiles and wherein there is no longer Jew or Gentile but only men supernaturally called to be of God's race.

The chronology of the events described in the Acts and of

the life of Saint Paul is sure only in its main outline and admits of variations in detail, which, however, are of no great import. Following herein the scholarship which seems to me to be the best founded, I, together with the editors of the Westminster Version, would assign the first general persecution and the death of Stephen to the year 36, three years after the Crucifixion.

There rose up some from the synagogue called that of the Freedmen and from the synagogues of the Cyrenaeans and Alexandrians, and of those of Cilicia and Asia [Cilicia, native country of Saul], disputing with Stephen. . . . And they stirred up the people and the elders and the scribes, and they came upon him and seized him, and took him before the council [the Sanhedrin]. And they brought forward false witnesses. . . . Then all who were sitting in the council [and Saul was among them] gazed at him, and they saw his face to be as the face of an angel. [Acts vi. 9-15.]

Stephen spoke, and Saul heard what he said. Stephen rehearsed the history of Israel and its infidelities, until the days of David,

who found favour before God, and asked that he might " provide a dwelling-place for the God of Jacob ; but it was Solomon who built him a house." [1] Yet the Most High dwelleth not in what is made of hand, as saith the prophet :

> " The heaven is my throne,
>   the earth the footstool of my feet ;
>   What manner of house shall ye build me, saith the Lord,
>   or what shall be the place of my resting ?
>   Did not my hand make all this ? " [2]

" Stiff of neck, uncircumcised of heart and ear, ye always resist the Holy Spirit ; as did your fathers, so do ye. Which of the prophets did not your fathers persecute ? And they killed those who proclaimed beforehand the coming of the just one, of whom now ye are become the betrayers and murderers, ye who have received the Law promulgated by angels, and have not kept it."

Now upon hearing these things they were cut to the heart, and gnashed their teeth at him. And being full of the Holy Spirit, he gazed at the heaven and saw the glory of God, and Jesus standing at the

---

[1] I (III) Kings vi. 1-2.   [2] Isa. lxvi. 1-2.

right hand of God ; and he said, " Behold, I see the heavens opened, and the Son of Man standing on the right hand of God."

But they cried out with a loud voice, and stopped their ears, and with one accord rushed upon him ; and they cast him out of the city and stoned him. And the witnesses laid down their garments at the feet of a young man called Saul. And while they were stoning Stephen, he prayed and said, " Lord Jesus, receive my spirit."

And falling upon his knees, he cried out with a loud voice, " Lord, lay not this sin to their charge."

And after saying this he fell asleep. And Saul was consenting to his death. [Acts vii. 46–viii. 1.]

Saul had his share of responsibility for the murder of Stephen. He kept the garments of them who stoned him. Although the word (νεανίας, a young man) used by Luke seems to suggest that Saul was only just emerging from adolescence, it is presumed that he was then about thirty-five.[1] In this case we can believe him to have been a member—the youngest— of the Sanhedrin. Stephen had been stoned in virtue of a disposition of the Law. And Saul had heard him cry out : " You who have created the Law, and have not kept the Law."

Here is a central theme of the future teaching of Saint Paul. Saul meditated the last words of Stephen ; the judging of Stephen and his death must have troubled his heart and perhaps have roused in him those thoughts which are so profound that one can scarcely avow them to oneself.

Paul's Conversion

The first general persecution of the Christians began with the murder of Stephen. Except for the Apostles, all those at Jerusalem scattered over Judaea and Samaria. " Saul was devastating the Church, entering into house after house, drag- ging away men and women and committing them to prison." " They who were scattered abroad went about preaching the word of the Gospel " [Acts viii. 3–4]. The deacon Philip preached to the Samaritans—the Samaritans whom the Jews scorned and contact with whom was for them impure. For

[1] Cf. Abbot Chapman in the *Journal of Theological Studies*, vol. ix. p. 59, Oct 1907.

the first time the Gospel was spreading over the Gentiles. Peter and John came to Samaria, and laid their hands upon those who had been baptized, in order that they might receive the Holy Spirit.

But Saul, still breathing threat and slaughter against the disciples of the Lord, approached the high priest and asked of him letters to the synagogues in Damascus, that if he found any that were of the Way, whether men or women, he might bring them bound to Jerusalem. And as he journeyed, it befell that he was nearing Damascus, when suddenly a light from heaven flashed about him, and he fell to the earth, and heard a voice saying to him, " Saul, Saul, why dost thou persecute me ? "

But he said, " Who art thou, Lord ? "

And he said, " I am Jesus, whom thou dost persecute. But arise and go into the city, and it shall be told thee what thou must do."

Now the men who were travelling with him were standing speechless, hearing the sound, but beholding no one. And Saul arose from the ground, but when his eyes were opened, he saw nothing ; and they led him by the hand and brought him into Damascus. And he was three days without seeing, and he neither ate nor drank.

Now there was in Damascus a certain disciple called Ananias ; and the Lord said to him in a vision, " Ananias ! " And he said, " Behold me, Lord." And the Lord said to him, " Arise, and go into the street which is called Straight, and seek in the house of Judas one Saul, from Tarsus ; for behold, he prayeth."

(And Paul saw a man called Ananias enter and lay hands upon him, that he might see.)

But Ananias answered, " Lord, I have heard from many about this man, and of all the evil that he hath done to thy saints in Jerusalem ; and here, too, he hath authority from the high priests to bind all that call upon thy name."

But the Lord said to him, " Go, for this man is a vessel chosen by me, to bear my name before nations and kings and the children of Israel. For I will show him how much he must undergo for my name."

So Ananias departed, and entered the house, and laying his hands upon him, he said, " Brother Saul, the Lord hath sent me—even Jesus, who appeared to thee upon thy journey hither—in order that thou mayest recover thy sight, and be filled with the Holy Spirit."

And straightway there fell from his eyes as it were scales, and he recovered his sight, and stood up and was baptized ; after which he took food and regained his strength.   [Acts ix. 1-19.]

The moment of Paul's conversion is also the moment he received his mission : he is chosen to bear the name of Jesus before nations and kings and the children of Israel. And the great doctrine he is to preach, according to which the faithful compose one body, which is the mysterious body of Jesus, continuing through time the work of the ransom of men, is already stated in the words he had heard : " I am Jesus, whom thou dost persecute."

Paul's Missions

Paul's conversion took place the same year as the martyrdom of Stephen—hence in the year 36, according to the chronology I am following. He at once set about spreading the Gospel, withdrew for a time into Arabia, then returned to Damascus, preaching Jesus in the synagogues. The zealots of Israel laid wait for him and wished to kill him. It was then that his disciples took him and let him down by night through the wall, lowering him in a basket.

He goes to Jerusalem to see Peter. This former persecutor is at first suspected ; it is Barnabas who helps him overcome this suspicion, and leads him to Peter and James. At Jerusalem he preaches to the Jews who speak Greek. Then suddenly he leaves, after seeing a vision in the temple which enlightens him concerning his mission, and to which he will allude eighteen years later, at the time of his last visit to the holy city.

He remained some years " in the regions of Syria and Cilicia." During this time Peter (after the vision of the great sheet, knit at the four corners, descending from heaven, whereon were all manner of four-footed beasts, both pure and impure, which from thenceforth he had permission to eat) baptized the centurion Cornelius and established the rule that pagans could be baptized. At Antioch was established the first church made up of Jews and Gentiles, wherein the Gentiles doubtless formed the majority (it was there that the disciples were first called " Christians "). Barnabas, sent from Jerusalem to supervise the work thus begun, goes to seek Paul at Tarsus and brings him with him to Antioch. There they spent a year (42–43), teaching a considerable multitude. New revelations continue to instruct Paul. He then goes, for the second time after his conversion, to Jerusalem (44), in company with Barnabas, as a result of a prediction of a general famine, in order to bring relief to the faithful of Judaea. Thereafter both return to Antioch.

It is from thence that he departed with Barnabas for his first mission journey (47–48), sent by the church of Antioch. They went to Cyprus, Barnabas' native land, then to Antioch in Pisidia, where they were received with enthusiasm by a population made up of Anatolians, of Greeks and of Jews. Paul tells the synagogue of the remission of sins by Christ : " In him everyone that believeth is justified from all those things from which ye could not be justified by the Law of Moses." But confronted with the bitter opposition then shown by the Jews, Paul and Barnabas cry out : " To you it was necessary that the word of God should be spoken first ; since ye thrust him from you, and judge yourselves unworthy of everlasting life, behold we turn to the Gentiles " [Acts xiii. 47]. Here is a threat which Paul will several times repeat, but which will not prevent him from continuing still to preach to the Jews. At Lystra, whither they next journey, the crowds take Barnabas for Jupiter, because of his tall stature, and Paul for Mercury, " because it was he that took the lead in speech " [Acts xiv. 13]. Then, persuaded by Jews come from Antioch in Pisidia and from Iconium, the people stoned Paul.

Once returned to Antioch in Syria, Paul soon left for a third visit to Jerusalem. His purpose was to confer with " the pillars," Peter, James and John, and he had to defend himself against the accusations of the Judaizers, who asserted that without the circumcision prescribed by the Law one could not be saved. (During this period the Christian Jews continued for their part in fact to follow the Mosaic observances. The Judaizers considered that a necessity, required by God, and consequently wished to subject to circumcision the faithful who came from among the Gentiles.) The " pillars " vested Paul and Barnabas with their authority, Peter and James caused the council of Jerusalem (49) to recognize the special mission of these two to preach to the Gentiles, just as the mission of the apostles living in Judaea was to preach to the Jews. Christians come from among the Gentiles shall only be held, with regard to observances common with the Jews, to abstain from meats offered to idols (a measure which was to protect converts against the dangers of pagan contamination) ; and also, in order that a common life with their Jewish brethren might be possible, from the flesh of strangled animals and from blood. Paul and Barnabas returned to Antioch, where the whole Christian community rejoiced at the letter which they brought from Jerusalem, which confirmed the freedom of the Gentiles.

For his second mission journey (49–52) Paul separated from Barnabas who, taking John Mark as travelling companion, departs for Cyprus, while Paul takes with him Silas (Silvanus), a Roman citizen like himself. The first stops on their journey are Syria, Cilicia, Galatia, where they attach Timothy as a companion. Timothy was a young Greek born of a Jewish mother. Reluctantly, and to spare the feelings of the Judaeo-Christians, Paul circumcises him. All three then go on to Macedonia ; at Philippi they are cast into prison and baptize their jailor ; at Thessalonica, capital of the province, over-zealous Jews accuse them of defying the decrees of Caesar, because they say " that there is another king, one Jesus " ; which implied not only danger to public order, but treason against the imperial cult (*laesa majestas*). At Beroea the synagogue welcomes their preaching with all eagerness, " examining daily the scriptures, to see whether these things were so." Driven out once more, they pass over into Achaia. Paul arrives in Athens.

While Paul awaited Silas and Timothy at Athens,

his spirit was vexed within him at beholding the city full of idols. He reasoned therefore in the synagogue with the Jews and with them that worshipped, and in the *agora* (the market place) every day with the chance comers. And some of the Epicurean and Stoic philosophers engaged in discussions with him; and some said, "What would this prater say ? " But others, " He seemeth to be an announcer of foreign gods " : this because he proclaimed Jesus and the resurrection. And they took and brought him unto the Hill of Ares, saying, " May we know what is this new teaching uttered by thee ? For thou bringest some strange things to our ears ; we wish therefore to know what these things mean."

Now all Athenians and the foreign residents had leisure for naught save to tell or hear something new. [Acts xvii. 16-21.]

Here is Paul's discourse in the midst of the Hill of Ares :

" Men of Athens, I behold you in all respects not a little religious. For as I was passing along and noticing the objects of your worship, I found also an altar bearing the inscription, *To the unknown god.* What therefore ye worship in ignorance, that I proclaim to you. ' God, who made the world and all things therein, he, being lord of heaven and earth,' [1] dwelleth not in temples made with hands, neither hath he need of aught that he should be served by human hands, seeing that himself ' giveth ' to all life and ' breath ' and all things. Yea, from one man he hath made the whole human race to dwell upon the entire face of the earth, determining their appointed seasons and the boundaries of their abode, that they should seek God, if haply groping after him they might find him. Not that he is far from any one of us ; for in him

we live and move and have our being,
as also some of your poets [2] have said,
For we are his very offspring.

Being therefore the offspring of God, we ought not to think that the divine is like to gold or silver or stone, to aught graven by art and invention of man. Such times of ignorance God hath overlooked, but doth now declare to men that all are everywhere to repent, inasmuch as he hath appointed a day whereon he is about ' to judge the world with justice ' [3] by the man whom he hath determined, giving proof thereof to all by raising him from the dead." [Acts xvii. 22-31.]

But when the Athenians heard him speak of the resurrection of the dead, " some jeered while others said : ' We shall hear thee about this yet again ' " [Acts xvii. 32].

Paul soon moved on to Corinth. He spent eighteen months there (51-52), practising with Aquila and Priscilla the trade of tent maker, preaching each Saturday in the synagogue and convincing a great number, but constantly encountering contradiction and opposition. In this city so typical of the Graeco-Roman world, he proclaimed the Gospel of the Cross, without troubling himself as to whether he offended

---

[1] Isa. xlii. 5.   [2] Epimenides and Aratus.
[3] Ps. ix. 8 (9) ; Ps. xcvi. (xcv.) 13 ; xcviii. (xcvii.) 9.

both Jewish pride and Greek reason. His ministry, undertaken " in weakness, and in fear, and in much trembling," was especially fruitful. " Fear not," the Saviour said to him, " but speak and hold not thy peace, because I am with thee, and no one shall set upon thee to hurt thee : for much people is mine in this city." It was from Corinth that he wrote his two Epistles to the Thessalonians.

He quit Corinth by sea for Ephesus, where an Alexandrian Jew named Apollos, one " powerful in the Scriptures," had already preached Jesus, and where Paul remained during three winters (52–53, 53–54, 54–55). The first Epistle to the Corinthians was written at Ephesus (55). It was at the end of Paul's residence at Ephesus that a certain Demetrius, a maker of silver shrines at Artemis, aroused a great disturbance against the Christians who had harmed his business. " Great is Artemis of the Ephesians," cried the people. This Demetrius was the precursor of many an expert in the art of arousing great economico- or politico-mystical movements.

Paul then began his third great journey. He returned into Macedonia, from whence he sent to the Corinthians his second Epistle (55) and into Greece—probably at Corinth—whence he wrote his Epistles to the Galatians and to the Romans (56). Then he set sail again for Asia Minor. At Troas he brought back to life the young Eutychus who, falling asleep on the sill of a window while Paul preached, had tumbled from the third story. At last he felt moved once more to go to Jerusalem, " constrained in spirit," and not knowing what things should befall him therein, " save only that the Holy Spirit testifieth unto me in city after city, saying that bonds and afflictions await me."

" But I hold not my life of any account, that it should be dear unto me, if only I may accomplish my course, and the ministry which I have received from the Lord Jesus, to testify the gospel of the grace of God.

" And now, behold, I know that ye shall see my face no longer, all ye among whom I went about preaching the kingdom. . . . The silver or gold or clothing of none have I coveted ; yourselves know that to my own needs and to those with me these hands have ministered. In all things I have given you an example, how that toiling thus we must succour the weak, and remember the words of the Lord Jesus, who himself said, ' It is more blessed to give than to receive.' " [Acts xx. 24-25 ; 33-35.]

The elders of the church of Ephesus, whom he had caused to come to Miletus to take leave of them, fell upon Paul's neck and kissed him and escorted him to the ship.

At Caesarea, where he and his companions disembarked, a man moved by the spirit of prophecy takes Paul's girdle and binds with it his own hands and feet, saying : " Thus saith the Holy Spirit : So shall the Jews bind at Jerusalem the man whose is this girdle, and they shall deliver him into the hands of the gentiles." The Christians wished to restrain Paul from going, but he answered them : " What are ye doing, thus weeping and breaking my heart ? I am ready not only to be bound, but to die at Jerusalem for the name of the Lord Jesus " [Acts xxi. 10-13].

He arrived at Jerusalem (56) in time for the Jewish feast of Pentecost, prepared to celebrate it with all the people of Jerusalem. He was in great danger ; at once he was warned thereof by James and the elders. The Judaizing Christians were indignant at his apostolate among the uncircumcised. Upon the advice of James, Paul, in order to show his respect for the Law, went up to the Temple to purify himself along with four other men who had made a vow. But when the seven days of the purification were about to be completed, the Jews of Asia having seen him in the Temple, stirred up the multitude and

laid hands upon him, crying out, " Men of Israel, help ! This is the man who teacheth all everywhere against the people and the Law and this place, yea, and he hath brought Greeks into the temple, and hath defiled this holy place ! "

For they had previously seen Trophimus the Ephesian in the city with him, and they thought that Paul had brought him into the temple. And the whole city was moved, and there was a concourse of the people, and laying hold of Paul they dragged him out of the temple, and straightway the gates were closed. They were seeking to kill him when word was taken up to the tribune of the cohort that all Jerusalem was in an uproar. At once he took soldiers and centurions and ran down upon them ; and they, when they saw the tribune and the soldiers, left off beating Paul. Then the tribune came up and laid hold of him, and ordered him to be bound with two chains, and enquired who he was, and what he had done. Some in the crowd shouted back one thing, and others another ; and since he could not obtain sure knowledge by reason of the tumult, he ordered him to be brought into the fort. And when Paul came to the steps, he was actually being carried by the soldiers because of the violence of the crowd ; for the multitude of the people followed, crying out, " Away with him ! " [Acts xxi. 28–36.]

Paul then spoke, in Hebrew (Aramaic), recalling his education by Gamaliel and his zeal for the Law of Moses and how he had persecuted the Christians and how he had been converted. And referring to his first visit to Jerusalem after his conversion, he added:

And it befell me, after I had returned to Jerusalem and was praying in the temple, that I fell into an ecstasy, and saw him saying to me, " Make haste and go forth quickly from Jerusalem ; for they will not accept thy witness about me."
And I said, " Lord, themselves do know that I was imprisoning and beating throughout the synagogues those who believed in thee ; and when the blood of Stephen thy witness was shed, I myself was standing by and consenting and keeping the garments of them that slew him."
And he said to me, " Go ; for I shall send thee forth afar unto the gentiles." [Acts xxii. 17–21.]

" Away with such a fellow from the earth," answered the zealots, shouting and casting away their garments and throwing dust into the air. The tribune then ordered him to be brought into the fort, giving orders that he should be examined under the scourge. But when they had tied him down with the thongs, Paul said to the centurion who was standing by, " Is it lawful for you to scourge a man that is a Roman, and uncondemned ? "

When the centurion heard this, he went to the tribune and reported it, saying, " What art thou about to do ? This man is a Roman."
Then the tribune came and said to him, " Tell me, art thou a Roman ? "
And he said, " Yea."

And the tribune answered, " I obtained this citizenship at a great price."

And Paul said, " But I was born thereto."

At once therefore they that were to examine him departed from him ; and the tribune was afraid when he realized that Paul was a Roman, because he had bound him. [Acts xxii. 26–29.]

The next day the Sanhedrin met, and Paul, knowing that it was divided between the Sadducees and the Pharisees, cried out :

" Brethren, I am a Pharisee, the son of Pharisees ; it is about the hope and the resurrection of the dead that I am being judged ! "

When he said this, a dispute arose between the Pharisees and Sadducees, and the multitude was divided. For the Sadducees say that there is no resurrection, nor yet angel or spirit, but the Pharisees confess all these. So a great uproar ensued, and some of the scribes belonging to the party of the Pharisees stood up and fought the question, saying, " We find no evil in this man ; what if a spirit have spoken to him, or an angel ? "

And whereas the dispute was waxing hot, the tribune, fearing lest Paul should be torn to pieces by them, ordered the troops to come down and carry him off from the midst of them, and bring him into the fort. And the following night the Lord stood by him and said, " Be of good courage ; for as thou hast borne witness about me in Jerusalem, so thou must bear witness also in Rome." [Acts xxiii. 6–11.]

* * *

Some forty fanatics then took an oath not to eat or drink until they should have killed Paul. Paul's nephew, having heard of this scheme, warned the tribune that the schemers would come and ask him to hale Paul over once more before the Sanhedrin, so as thus to find opportunity to kill him on the road. Whereupon the tribune caused Paul to be carried with a sufficient guard to Caesarea, where he was placed in the hands of Felix, the governor.

Five days later the high priest Ananias, with some of the elders and a certain pleader called Tertullus, arrived at Caesarea in order to accuse Paul before the governor. Paul said once again that he was innocent, and that he was accused only because he taught the resurrection of the dead. Felix, who had heard talk concerning what the Christians believed, adjourned the case, and held Paul in prison for two years (56-58) ; he went often to converse with him, to discuss religious questions and because he hoped also that money would be given him by his prisoner as the price of being set free. Then Felix was replaced by Fortius Festus ; and wishing to gain favour with the Jews, he left Paul in bonds.

After several days the new Governor caused Paul to appear before his tribunal. To make himself pleasing to the men of the Temple, who continued to raise against Paul all sorts of accusations, the Governor proposed to him that the case be carried to Jerusalem. That would have meant the end of Paul. It was then that he appealed to Caesar.

" Thou hast appealed to Caesar ? To Caesar thou shalt go," answered Festus.

A few days later King Agrippa (Herod Agrippa II) and his sister Bernice came to welcome Festus. He spoke to them of Paul, being careful (which was good Roman propaganda, and after all not untrue) to add that he had replied to the Jews who requested Paul's condemnation, " that it was not the custom of the Romans thus to make a present of a man before the accused had met his accusers face to face, and had been given the opportunity of defence against the charge." Thus Roman law and the law-mindedness of pagan civilization protected the apostle against the fury of Israel's theocracy gone astray.

His curiosity aroused, Agrippa asked to hear Paul. And the next day Paul was brought before Agrippa and Bernice, who had entered with great ceremony into the hall of audience, together with the tribunes and prominent men of the city. Once more Paul stated his defence, going into detail, for he knew that the King was well posted with regard to the customs and controversies of the Jews. Once more he told the story of his conversion, adding this detail, that at a moment when a light brighter than that of the sun came down from heaven upon him and his companions, all the latter fell to the ground with him, and that the words spoken to him from Heaven were said in Aramaic :

" Having therefore received until this day the help which is from God, I stand testifying both to small and great, asserting nothing beyond

3

what the prophets and Moses said was to befall : how that the Christ
was to suffer, how rising from the dead he was to be the first to proclaim
light both to the people and to the gentiles."

While he was thus making his defence, Festus saith with a loud voice,
" Thou art mad, Paul ; thy much learning is turning thee to madness."

But Paul saith, " I am not mad, Excellent Festus, but I am uttering
words of sober truth. For the king knoweth about these things, to
whom also I am speaking freely. I am persuaded that none of these
things hath escaped him ; for all this hath not been done in a corner.
Believest thou the prophets, King Agrippa ? I know that thou believest
them."

But Agrippa said to Paul, " Thou thinkest it is a small matter to make
me a Christian ! "

And Paul answered, " I would to God that both in small matter and
in great, not only thou, but all who hear me to-day might become such
as I am, excepting these bonds ! "

And the king arose, and the governor and Bernice and those that
had been seated with them ; and after they had withdrawn they spoke
with one another, saying, " This man doth naught deserving death or
bonds."

And Agrippa said to Festus, " This man might have been released,
if he had not appealed to Caesar." [Acts xxvi. 22-32.]

The last remark of Herod Agrippa was, as has been pointed
out, tragically ironic. Paul was on his way to Nero, to new
captivities, until he should meet death.

He had spoken in his own defence without fear and without
bravado, with that moderation and prudence of which those
charged with great tasks should give proof, and with great
respect for that holy Law which he venerated and of whose
regimen he was charged to proclaim the end, and with a pathetic
care not to bring about a final break with the authorities of
the Temple. Now that break had been consummated.

He was taken away by sea, bound for Italy. Luke, who
accompanied him, reports in detail this long and dramatic
journey. From a tiny port called " Fair Havens " in Crete,
wherein they were for some time detained by bad weather,
they tried, against Paul's advice, to reach another place to
spend the winter, and were shipwrecked near the island of
Malta. Passengers and crew—in all two hundred and seventy-
six souls—were all saved, as Paul had promised (an Angel had

said to him : God has given to you all those who sail with you). As the shipwrecked men were warming themselves at a fire they had built near the shore, a poisonous snake crawled out of the fagots and bit Paul's hand. Whereupon the natives of the place cried out, " This man is certainly a murderer ; for though he has escaped from the sea, justice has not suffered him to live." But when they saw Paul shake off into the fire the beast which hung from his finger, and suffer no evil therefrom, they thought he was a god.

Paul and his companions remained in Malta for the three winter months. Then, embarking on an Alexandrian ship, they crossed over to Syracuse, then to Rhegium (Reggio) and to Puteoli (Puzzuoli) ; from thence they continued to Rome (in the year 59), where the Christian community was already well established. The Christians came to meet them, as far as the market of Appius and the Three Taverns (thirty or forty miles from the city), at whose sight Paul gave thanks to God and took courage. In Rome he was allowed to live by himself together with the soldier who guarded him.

Luke's narrative stops with the mention of the fact that Paul abode for two whole years in a hired lodging of his own, receiving all who came to him and evangelizing them. It was during the year 61 that he sent to the Ephesians, to the Colossians, to Philemon, to the Philippians the Epistles called those of his captivity. The Epistle to the Hebrews likewise was written during his years of captivity at Rome. All the substance of this admirable scriptural dissertation, in which all Jewish science is drawn upon to prove the advent of the New Law, is surely and directly from Paul. Nevertheless its style indicates, to the minds of most exegetes, the hand of another writer, most likely a disciple himself well versed in the Scriptures whom Paul was instructing in his place of detention and who would later have elaborated on the notes then taken. Yet it seems to me not an impossible hypothesis that the imprisoned apostle, using all the skill at his command, may have himself composed a controversial treatise very different as to style from the hastily dictated letters to the various churches.

It is believed that Paul was released at the end of the year 61. In 64 took place the burning of Rome, and the persecution of

Nero began. It is possible that Paul had at this moment undertaken a fourth missionary voyage, this time to Macedonia, from whence he wrote his Epistle to Titus and his first Epistle to Timothy. It is further supposed that his second captivity in Rome lasted from 66 to 67, and that in the latter year he wrote his second letter to Timothy, and that it was in the same year that he was put to death, probably at the place known to-day as the Three Fountains.

CHAPTER II

THE APOSTOLATE

Paul's Mission

"THE SPIRITS OF THE PROPHETS ARE SUBJECT TO THE prophets." Paul had an extremely clear and profound consciousness of his mission. He knows that he can do nothing by himself, but that God, by the very fact that He gives him a mission, makes him suited to that mission. That is why he can bear witness to himself.

Thanks be to God who at all times leadeth us in triumph in Christ, and through us maketh manifest the savour of the knowledge of him in every place. For we are the fragrance of Christ unto God in regard of them that are being saved and them that are perishing ; to these a savour from death unto death ; but to those a savour from life unto life. And for such things who is sufficient ? We indeed do not, as so many, make a trade of the word of God ; but we speak in Christ, as out of a sincere heart, as sent from God and in his presence. [2 Cor. ii. 14-17.]

Nay, ye are our epistle, written in our hearts, known and read by all men. Manifestly ye are an epistle of Christ, drawn up by us, written not with ink but with the Spirit of the living God, not on " tablets of stone " but on " tablets that are hearts of flesh." [1]

Such is the confidence we have through Christ towards God. Not as though we were of ourselves sufficient to think anything, as from ourselves, but our sufficiency is from God. He it is that hath made us competent ministers of the new covenant, not of the letter but of the spirit ; for the letter killeth, but the spirit quickeneth.

Now if the ministration of death, that was graven in letters upon stones, was inaugurated in such glory that the children of Israel were unable to look steadfastly upon the face " of Moses, by reason of the glory of his face "—a glory that was to pass away—shall not the ministration of the spirit be yet more glorious ? For if the ministration of condemnation was glorious, much more doth the ministration of justification abound in glory. For though the former was made

---

[1] Cf. Exod. xxxi. 18 ; Prov. iii. 3 ; Ezek. xi. 19.

glorious ; yet in this regard it is without glory, by reason of the over-whelming glory of the latter. For if that which was but passing had glory, much more shall that which abideth be glorious. [2 Cor. iii. 2-11.]

It is to the Gentiles that Paul is sent.

Seeing that I was entrusted with the gospel for the uncircumcised as was Peter with that for the circumcised, (for he who hath wrought in Peter unto the apostolate of the circumcised hath wrought in me also unto the gentiles), and recognizing the grace conferred upon me, James and Cephas and John—they that were reputed as pillars—gave to Barnabas and myself the right hand of fellowship, we to go to the gentiles, they to the circumcised. [Gal. ii. 7-9.]

Aware at once of his weakness as a man and of the power of grace, the Apostle is free of all save only God. He chastises his body, he is quit of himself, he is handed over to tribulations. He is given to all. And while he lives only for the Gospel, he aspires to die in order to be with Jesus.

Am I not free ? Am I not an Apostle ? Have I not seen Jesus our Lord ? Are not you my work in the Lord ? [1 Cor. ix. 1.]
Woe to me if I preach not the Gospel. [1 Cor. ix. 16.]
When we came to Macedonia our flesh had no rest, but in everything we were afflicted ; combats without, fears within. . . . [2 Cor. vii. 5.]
We preach not ourselves ; but Christ Jesus as Lord, and ourselves merely as your slaves for Jesus' sake. It is God who said, " Out of dark-ness shall shine light," that hath shone in our hearts, unto the illuminating knowledge of the glory of God, in the person of Christ.
Still we hold this treasure in earthen vessels, that so the grandeur of the power may be God's and not from us. Pressed on every side, yet not crushed ; perplexed, yet not unto despairing ; hard driven yet not deserted ; struck down, yet not destroyed—ever we bear about in our body the dying of Jesus, so that the life, too, of Jesus may be made manifest in our bodies. For we who live are ever being delivered up to death for Jesus' sake, so that the life, too, of Jesus may be made manifest in our mortal flesh. Thus in us death worketh ; but in you, life. Yet since we have the same spirit of faith as shown in that which is written,
I have believed, therefore have I spoken,[1]
We too believe, and therefore speak. [2 Cor. iv. 5-13.]
Whereas I am in all respects free, I have enslaved myself to all men,

---

[1] Ps. cxvl. 10 (cxv. 1).

that I may gain the more of them. And I have become to the Jews as a Jew, that I may gain Jews ; to them under the Law, as under the Law (albeit not myself under the Law), that I may gain those under the Law ; to those outside the Law (I too) as outside the Law (not that I am outside the law of God, for I am within the law of Christ) that I may gain those outside the Law. To the weak I have become weak, that I may gain the weak ; I have become all things to all men, that at all costs I may save some. And all things I do for the sake of the gospel, that I too may have part therein.

Know ye not that they who run in the race all run indeed, but one receiveth the prize ? So run ye as to make it yours. Now every competitor restraineth himself in all things—they, to be sure, to receive a perishable crown, but we an imperishable. I therefore run, yet not aimlessly ; I fight, not as beating the air : but I bruise my body and bring it into bondage, lest haply after being herald to others I myself become rejected. [1 Cor. ix. 19-27.]

To me it is a very small matter to be put in trial by you or by man's day, nay, I put not mine own self on trial. For I know naught against myself, yet am I not thereby acquitted, but he that trieth me is the Lord. [1 Cor. iv. 3-4.]

Is it then with men I would find favour or with God ? Or is it men I ask to please ? If I were still pleasing men, I should not be a servant of Christ. [Gal. i. 10.]

To me to live is Christ, and to die is gain. But if to live in the flesh meaneth for me fruitful labour—then, which I am to choose I cannot tell. I am caught between the two ; my longing is to dissolve and to be with Christ—for that were far better—yet for your sakes to remain in the flesh is more needful. [Philip. i. 21-24.]

Paul's Apology

Paul cherished with a peerlessly strong and tender love all those whom he led into the faith. His heart is torn when he feels them to be threatened by the teaching of false doctors, especially when he sees them tempted to forget the freedom which he taught them, or to misinterpret it. He needs their confidence ; he has not the right to allow himself to be slandered in their hearts ; he is forced, by his love of them, to make his apology before them.

In times past, to be sure, because ye knew not God, ye were enslaved to what are not really gods ; but now that ye have come to know God, or rather have come to be known by God, how can ye turn back again to the weak and beggarly elements [1] where ye wish to be enslaved once again ? Ye observe days, and months, and seasons, and years ! I am afraid of you, lest perchance I have toiled among you in vain. [Gal. iv. 8–11.]

Ye know that it was owing to sickness of the flesh that I formerly preached to you, and that which was your trial in my flesh ye despised not, nor loathed, nay, ye received me as an angel of God, as Christ Jesus. Where then is your self-congratulation ? Yea, I bear you witness that, if it had been possible, ye had plucked out your eyes and given them to me. Am I, then, become your enemy, because I tell you the truth ? . . . My little children, of whom I am again in travail, until Christ be formed in you. [Gal. iv. 13–16, 19.]

We became babes in the midst of you ; yearning over you, like a nurse cherishing her children, we were minded to share with you, not only the gospel of God, but also our own lives—so dear to us had ye become. [1 Thess. ii. 7–8.]

Not to shame you do I write thus, but as my beloved children to admonish you. For though you have ten thousand tutors in Christ, yet you have not many fathers ; for in Christ Jesus I begot you through the gospel. I beseech you, therefore, take pattern from me, as I from Christ. [1 Cor. iv. 14–16.]

Look at those dogs, look at those evil workers, look at those mutilators ! For *we* are the circumcision, who worship by the spirit of God, whose boast is in Christ Jesus, and who do not trust in the flesh. And yet for my part I have grounds for trust even in the flesh. If any man deemeth that he can trust in the flesh, better can I—circumcised when eight days old, of the race of Israel, of the tribe of Benjamin, a Hebrew born of Hebrews, in observance of the Law a Pharisee, in zeal a persecutor of the Church, in the justness to be found in the Law, proved without blame.

But such things as were to my gain, these for Christ I have come to count as loss. Nay, more, I count all things loss by reason of the excellence of the knowledge of Christ Jesus my Lord. For his sake I have suffered the loss of all things and count them but dung, in order that I may gain Christ and be found in him, not having for my justness that which is from the Law, but that which is through faith in Christ, that justness which cometh from God, [based] upon faith. That so that I may know him, what the power of his resurrection, what fellowship in his sufferings, and become one with him in his death, in the

---

[1] On the " weak and beggarly elements," see below, p. 48.

hope that I may attain to the resurrection from the dead. Not that I
have already secured this, or am already made perfect. Rather I press on,
in the hope that I may lay hold of that for which Christ hath laid hold
of me. Brethren, I do not count myself to have laid hold of it already.
Yet one thing I do ; I forget what is behind, and strain forward to what
is before, and press on towards the goal, to gain the reward of God's
heavenly call in Christ Jesus. [Philip. iii. 2–14.]

Would that ye could bear with me in a little foolishness ! Nay,
bear with me ! For I am jealous for you with a jealousy divine. . . .
I esteem myself in no way to have fallen short of the most eminent
apostles. For though perchance unskilled in speech, yet am I not in
knowledge ; but in every respect and among all men have we manifested
it to you. . . .

What I do, that I shall continue to do, so that I may cut away the
occasion from them that seek an occasion, desiring in that wherein
they boast to be found even as we. For such as these are false apostles,
crafty workers, that disguise themselves as apostles of Christ. And no
wonder, for Satan himself disguiseth himself as an angel of light ;
it is no great thing, then, if his ministers too disguise themselves as
ministers of justness. But their end shall be according to their works.

I say it again—let none think me foolish ! But even if ye do, then
accept me as foolish, that I too may boast a little. What I speak by
way of confident boasting, I speak not according to the Lord, but as
it were in foolishness. Since many boast according to the flesh, I too
will boast. For ye suffer fools gladly, being wise yourselves ! For
ye suffer it, if any man enslave you, if any man devour you, if any
man prey upon you, if any man is arrogant, if any man strike you in
the face ! I speak to my own dishonour, as though we had shown ourselves weak in this regard ! Yet, in whatsoever any man is bold, I too
—I say it in foolishness—I too am bold ! They are Hebrews ? So
am I ! They are Israelites ? So am I ! They are the seed of Abraham ?
So am I ! They are ministers of Christ ? I—I speak as one beside himself—I am more : in labours more abundantly, in prisons more abundantly,
in stripes above measure, in deaths often. From the Jews five times did
I receive forty stripes save one, thrice was I beaten, once was I stoned,
thrice was I shipwrecked, by day and by night I was in the depths :
in journeyings often, in perils from rivers, perils from robbers, perils
from mine own nation, perils from the heathen, perils in city, perils
in wilderness, perils in the sea, perils from false brethren : in labour
and toil, in watchings often, in hunger and thirst, in fastings often,
in cold and nakedness : and besides all else, that which presseth on me
daily, my anxiety for all the churches ! Who is weak, and I am not

weak ? Who is made to stumble, and I am not on fire ? If I must needs boast, I will boast of mine infirmity ! The God and Father of our Lord Jesus Christ, who is blessed for evermore, knoweth that I lie not ! In Damascus the governor under King Aretas was guarding the city of the Damascenes in order to arrest me, but I was let down in a basket from a window in the wall, and I escaped his hands.

Must I needs boast ? True, it profiteth not—but I will come to the visions and revelations of the Lord. I know a man in Christ, who fourteen years ago—whether in the body, I know not, or out of the body, I know not, God knoweth—a man who was rapt to the third heaven. And of such a man I know—whether in the body or out of the body, I know not, God knoweth—that he was rapt to Paradise, and heard utterances unutterable, such as it is not permitted to man to speak. Of this same man will I boast ; but of myself I will not boast, save of mine infirmities ! For if I shall wish to boast, I shall not be foolish ; for I shall be speaking the truth. But I forbear, lest any man should think of me beyond what he seeth in me or heareth of me.

And lest I should be lifted up overmuch by the grandeur of these revelations, there was given me a thorn in my flesh, an angel of Satan to buffet me. About this thrice did I beseech the Lord that it might depart from me. And he hath said to me, " My grace is sufficient for thee, for strength is made perfect in infirmity." Most gladly, then, will I rather boast of mine infirmities, that so there may rest upon me the strength of Christ. Wherefore I am well content in infirmities, in insults, in hardships, in persecutions, in straits—for Christ's sake. For when I am weak, then I am strong. [2 Cor. xi. 1-2, 6, 12-33 ; xii. 1-10.]

There has been much discussion concerning the nature of that " thorn in my flesh " which Paul here mentions. Saint Gregory, in his *Moralia in Job*, wondered whether one should not understand thereby " the rebellion of the flesh." Everything seems, on the contrary, to indicate that we are here concerned with a physical illness which at intervals came to trouble him. The older writers (notably Saint Jerome and Saint Augustine) hazarded violent headaches. Among the modern, Lightfoot suggested epilepsy ; Ramsay, the most reasonable hypothesis of intermittent malaria. All of these hypotheses are, however, somewhat fruitless, for there are many ways in which sickness of body may " buffet " a man. What matters is the way in which a Saint knows how to understand them—

" for when I am weak, then I am strong "—and it is the imperishable phrase that Paul heard at such times : " My grace is sufficient for thee."

Paul as an Old Man

In his two letters to his faithful Timothy, the second written while he was in chains, the Apostle, having come to the end of his career, turns back a moment, considers the road he has travelled, and conveys to him whom he loves as a son the fruits of his own experience of wisdom and of suffering. One of the most beautiful of human things is the serenity of old workmen. The aged Paul has known all abandonment, his confidence is serene ; he knows that he has worked hard, and worked for God.

Now the aim of admonition is charity out of a pure heart and good conscience and faith unfeigned ; wherefrom some have erred, and have turned aside unto vain talking, wishing to be teachers of the Law, understanding neither what they say nor the things whereof they speak with such assurance. We know indeed that the Law is good, if a man use it lawfully, and if he know that a law is not framed for the just, but for the lawless and insubordinate, the impious and sinful, for the unholy and profane, for parricides and matricides, for murderers, for the impure, for sodomites, for kidnappers, for liars, for perjurers, and for whatever else is opposed to the sound doctrine. Such is the gospel of the glory of the blessed God, wherewith I have been entrusted. I give thanks to him who hath strengthened me, even to Christ Jesus our Lord, that he hath accounted me faithful, appointing me to the ministry, who was before a blasphemer and a persecutor and a wanton aggressor ; nevertheless I obtained mercy, because I acted out of ignorance, in unbelief. Indeed, the grace of our Lord abounded beyond measure, with the faith and the charity which are in Christ Jesus. Faithful is the saying, and worthy of all acceptance, that Christ Jesus came into the world to save sinners—of whom I am first ; but for this cause I obtained mercy, in order that in me first Christ Jesus might show forth all his longsuffering, as an example for those who should hereafter believe on him unto life everlasting.—[1 Tim. i. 5-16.]

I endure all things for the sake of the elect. [2 Tim. ii. 10.]

God hath not given us a spirit of cowardice, but a spirit of power and charity and discipline. Be not therefore ashamed of the witness to our Lord, nor of myself his prisoner ; but take thy share in suffering for the gospel, through the power of God. He it is that hath saved us and called us with a holy call, not in virtue of our works, but in virtue of his own purpose, and of the grace given us in Christ Jesus before times everlasting, but now manifested by the appearing of our Saviour Jesus Christ, who hath abolished death, but hath brought life and immortality to light through the gospel. Thereunto I have been appointed preacher and apostle and teacher : for the which reason also I am suffering these things : nevertheless I am not ashamed, for I know in whom I have put my trust, and I am confident that he is able to keep my deposit unto that day. Hold to the pattern of sound words which thou didst hear from me, in the faith and charity which are in Christ Jesus. Guard the good deposit, through the Holy Spirit who dwelleth in us. [2 Tim. i. 7–14.]

I adjure thee before God and Christ Jesus who is to judge living and dead, by his appearing and by his kingdom : preach the word, be urgent in season and out of season, reprove, rebuke, exhort, with all longsuffering and instruction. For there will come a time when men will not endure the sound doctrine, but following their own lusts will heap up to themselves teachers, to tickle their ears, and while refusing to listen to the truth, they will turn aside unto fables. But do thou be sober in all things, suffer hardship, do the work of evangelizing, fulfil thy ministry.

As for me, already I am poured out in sacrifice, and the time of my departure is at hand. I have fought the good fight, I have accomplished the course, I have kept the faith. For the rest there is laid up for me the crown of justness which the Lord, the just judge, shall award to me on that day, and not only to me, but to all who have loved his appearing. [2 Tim. iv. 1–8.]

Thou knowest that all in Asia turned away from me. [2 Tim. i. 15.]

This is doubtless a reference to certain Christians of Asia Minor who could have helped him at the time of his last imprisonment, and who abandoned him. At Rome, during the time of his first captivity, he was also left alone.

In my first defence no one came to my help : all forsook me : may it not be reckoned against them ! But the Lord stood by me and strengthened me, in order that through me the preaching of the gospel might be completed, and that all the gentiles might hear ; and I was delivered " from the lion's mouth." The Lord shall deliver me from every evil work, and shall save me unto his heavenly kingdom ; to him be the glory for ever and ever, Amen. [2 Tim. iv. 16–18.]

The Apostolic Life

No man militating for God becometh entangled in the affairs of the world. [2 Tim. ii. 4.]

To the Corinthians who confuse themselves with the game of futile controversies, some boasting of Apollos, some of Paul, and thus are settled in a kind of worldly wisdom, Paul recalls with flaming irony the true circumstances of apostolic life.

When one saith, " I am for Paul," and another, " I am for Apollos," are you not [simply] men ?
What then is Apollos ? What is Paul ? Ministers through whom you believed, even as to each the Lord gave power. I planted, Apollos watered, but God the while was making to grow. So then neither he that planteth is anything nor he that watereth, but God who maketh to grow. And he that planteth and he that watereth are but one, yet shall each receive his own reward according to his own toil. For we are God's fellow-workers, and ye are God's tillage, God's building. [1 Cor. iii. 4-9.]
Methinks God hath made display of us, the apostles, last of all, as men doomed to die—in that we are become a spectacle to the world, both to angels and to men. We are fools for Christ, but you are wise in Christ : we are weak, but you are strong : you have glory, but we dishonour. To this very hour we hunger and thirst and are naked and are buffeted, we are homeless and we toil, working with our own hands. We are reviled and we bless, we are persecuted and we endure, we are defamed and we answer softly ; we have become as the refuse of the world, the offscouring of all men, even to this hour ! [1 Cor. iv. 9-13.]

But it is in his second letter to the Church of Corinth that Paul draws the picture of the apostolic life, wherein the word overflows from the fulness of love and of contemplation.

For if we were beside ourselves—it was for God ; if we are sane— it is for you. For the charity of Christ constraineth us, since we judge thus, that one died for all—therefore all had died—and that he died for all that they who live may no longer live to themselves, but to him who died for them and was raised from the dead.
So that ourselves henceforward know no man according to the flesh. Nay, even if we have had knowledge of Christ according to

the flesh, yet now we have such knowledge of him no longer. If, then, any man be in Christ, he is a new creature : the former things have passed away : behold, all things are made new ! But all things are of God, who hath reconciled us to himself through Christ and hath given to us the ministry of reconciliation ; God, as it were, was reconciling the world to himself in Christ, by not reckoning against men their transgressions, and by the word of reconciliation wherewith he had entrusted us.

On Christ's behalf, then, we are ambassadors, God as it were exhorting through us ; we beseech you for Christ's sake, be reconciled to God ! Him that knew not sin, for our sakes he made sin, that in him we might become the justness of God.

Yea, as God's fellow-workers we exhort you not to receive the grace of God in vain. (For he saith,

> In an acceptable time have I heard thee,
> and in the day of salvation have I succoured thee.[1]

Behold, now is the truly acceptable time, behold, now is the day of salvation !) We give no offence in aught, that so the ministry be not blamed. But in everything we commend ourselves as the ministers of God, in much patience ; in tribulations, in hardships, in straits ; in stripes, in imprisonments, in tumults ; in labours, in watchings, in fastings ; in chastity, in knowledge, in longsuffering, in goodness, in the Holy Spirit, in charity unfeigned, in the word of truth, in the power of God ; with the armour of justness on the right hand and on the left, in glory and dishonour, in evil report and good report, as deceivers and yet truthful, as unknown and yet well known, as " dying and behold we live, as chastised and yet not done to death," as mourning yet ever rejoicing, as poor yet enriching many, as having naught yet possessing all things. [2 Cor. v. 13-21 ; vi. 1-10.]

Though walking in the flesh, we do not war according to the flesh, for the weapons of our warfare are not of the flesh, but powerful before God for the overthrow of strongholds ; yea, we overthrow reasonings and every lofty thing that exalteth itself against the knowledge of God, we bring every mind into captivity to the obedience of Christ. [2 Cor. x. 3-16.]

The word of God is not fettered. [2 Tim. ii. 9.]

The Wisdom of the World and the Wisdom of God

The wisdom proclaimed by Paul is not the wisdom of the philosophers, it is the wisdom of the saints. It is not the wisdom

---

[1] Isa. xlix. 8.

which may be acquired through the natural powers of the
reason, but that which is given by faith. Preaching a God
hung from the rood, Who triumphs over death by means of
death and Who reconciles all things in the racking torture of
the Cross ; announcing the beatitudes to the poor and eternal
life to all us sinners, and a love which frees from the law by
means of the law, this wisdom shocks at once the Jewish
expectation of a Messiah triumphing in the world and the
Greek refusal to bend the reason before the sanctity of God ;
this wisdom is a stumbling-block to everyone who measures
(which is folly indeed) things divine by a scale of the visible
and the human.

Christ hath sent me . . . to preach the gospel, not indeed with the
utterance of wisdom, lest the cross of Christ become void.
For the word of the cross is folly to those that are perishing, but to
us who are being saved it is the power of God. For it is written,
>   I will destroy the wisdom of the wise,[1]
>   And the prudence of the prudent I will set at nought.
Where is the man of wisdom ? Where is the scribe ? Where is the
disputant of this world ? Hath not God turned to folly the wisdom of
the world ? For whereas it was according to the wisdom of God that
the world by means of its wisdom should fail to know God, it is by
means of the preaching of folly that God hath thought well to save
them that believe. For the Jews demand signs and the Greeks seek after
wisdom ; but we—we preach Christ crucified, to the Jews a stumbling-
block, and to the gentiles folly, but to those who are called, whether
Jew or Greek, Christ the power of God and the wisdom of God. For
the folly of God is wiser than men, and stronger than men is his
weakness. [1 Cor. i. 17-25.]

He Who makes all things out of nothing chooses that which
is nothing in order to make something better than that which
is ; He chooses that which is sickly and foolish according to
the standard of this world, in order to build that which is wise
and strong according to the reality of God. And in this is
God's glory.

For, contemplate your own call, brethren ; not many of you are
wise according to the flesh, not many are powerful, not many of good

---

[1] Isa. xxix. 14.   The verse following has reminiscences of Isa. xix. 11-12 ;
xxxiii. 18.

birth. Nay, the foolish things of the world God hath chosen, so as to put to shame the men of wisdom, and the weak things of the world God hath chosen, so as to put to shame the strong things, and the base things of the world, aye, the things that are despised, the things that are not, God hath chosen, so as to bring to naught the things that are, lest any flesh should vaunt itself in the face of God. It is from him that ye have your being in Christ Jesus, in that he hath become to us wisdom God-imparted, yea, and justness and sanctification and redemption, so that, according as it is written :—

Let him who boasteth, boast in the Lord.[1] [1 Cor. i. 26–31.]

Jesus Christ is our wisdom. And Paul's action itself gives witness thereto, who wishes to know nothing but Jesus, and Jesus crucified, and who teaches with the power of the spirit and of miracles for proofs.

As for myself, brethren, when I came unto you, I came proclaiming to you the witness of God without exuberance of eloquence or wisdom. For I resolved to know nought among you save Jesus Christ, and him crucified. And in weakness and fear and much trembling came I unto you, and my discourse and my preaching were not set forth in captivating words of wisdom, but with plain evidence of the spirit and of power, that your faith might not rest on the wisdom of men, but on the power of God. [1 Cor. ii. 1–5.]

Paul never scorned reason or nature ; he knows that they are good and capable of attaining, even though in a fashion imperfect and precarious in fact, their appropriate ends, which are good and beautiful. If grace can raise up and sanctify nature, it is because nature is already in itself something good.

Every creature of God is good (καλόν). Nothing is to be rejected, so it be received with thanksgiving ; for it is sanctified by the word of God and by prayer. [1 Tim. iv. 4–5.]

By the natural road which common sense and which philosophy follow, the reason can know God, starting with visible things. And that for which Paul reproaches the wise men of this world is precisely that having known the existence of the true God, they closed their eyes to His sublime

[1] Jer. ix. 23–24.

unity, to His all-powerfulness and his incomprehensibility, which they could, and should, also have recognized, and they have bowed down to idols.

What is known about God is clear to them, for God himself hath made it clear. For since the creation of the world his invisible attributes—his everlasting power and divinity—are to be discerned and contemplated through his works, so that they are without excuse, inasmuch as having come to know God, they yet have not glorified him as God or rendered thanks, but they became vain in their reasonings and their senseless heart hath been darkened. [Rom. i. 19-21.]

But the mystery of our state is that our nature and our reason, as we see them in real and concrete existence, cannot by themselves alone attain the fulness and the perfection of that of which they are capable. All the more, if they set up to usurp that which is beyond their reach, they will become for us a snare, an occasion of sin and of death. With regard to eternal life and absolute wisdom, faith alone—and reason which heeds faith—truly knows the road.

As then ye have received Christ Jesus the Lord, so walk in him, rooted and built up in him, and established in the faith according as ye were taught abounding in thanksgiving.
See to it that there be no man making you his spoil by force of his philosophy and deceitful fancies, following the traditions of men, following the elements of the world, and not following Christ. [Colos. ii. 6-8.]

"Philosophy and deceitful fancies." The word *philosophy* is used in this passage in a rather improper sense, and designates the school of religious thought of the falsely wise Judaizers of Corinth. But that sense applies as well, we may rest confident, to philosophy such as our modern phenomenalists or positivists or Hegelians would have us know it.
As for the "elements of the world" of which Saint Paul here speaks (as he does in this same Epistle to the Colossians, ii. 20, and in the Epistle to the Galatians, iv. 4 and 9), Saint John Chrysostom thought these words referred to "the sun and the moon," to the extent that they determined the feasts of the Jewish calendar. Others believe, seemingly with better

4

reason, that they relate to the elemental forces of the cosmos
which the Judaizing "philosophers" contaminated as they
were with semi-gnostic ideas, confused with the angels. It
would appear that in any case it might be permitted in a more
general fashion to understand by these "weak and beggarly"
[Gal. iv. 9] elements of the world the created forces and causes
to which the mind enslaves itself when it seeks in them the
ultimate explanation of things and the supreme governance of
its feasts.

The true wisdom of eternal life is the contemplation of the
profundities of God, which the Spirit of God alone knows,
and of which, through faith and in faith, God causes a mysterious knowledge to come down upon us when we have reached
the perfect age of the Christian.

Nevertheless among the mature (*inter perfectos*) it is wisdom that
we speak, a wisdom, indeed, not of this world, nor of the rulers of
this world, who are tottering to their fall. Rather, we speak of the
wisdom of God embodied in a mystery, that hidden wisdom which God
devised before the ages unto our glory ; a wisdom which none of the
rulers of the world hath come to know—for had they known it, they
would not have crucified the Lord of glory. On the contrary, it is as
the Scripture saith :
What eye hath not seen, what ear hath not heard—what hath not
entered into heart of men—all these things God hath prepared for them
that love him.[1]
Yea, to us God hath revealed it through the Spirit, for the Spirit
exploreth all things, even the deep things of God. For who among
men knoweth what passeth in a man save the spirit of the man within
him ! Even so the things of God none hath come to know save the
Spirit of God. Now we have not received the spirit of the world, but
the Spirit which is from God, that we may realize the graces God hath
given us. And of these same we speak, not in words learnt of human
wisdom, but in those learnt of the Spirit. [1 Cor. ii. 6-13.]

The natural man, he who thinks and acts solely in accordance
with the natural energies of the soul giving life to the body,
and whose reason drowses in his senses, does not judge spiritual

---

[1] Cf. Isa. lxiv. 4, which is reproduced, not word for word, but in its general
drift. The words between dashes are added by Paul himself.

things by spiritual, but by carnal standards. He does not understand the things of God. But the spiritual man—he who lives in accordance with the powers of grace—awakened to the things of God by the spirit of God, possesses the standard by which all things can be judged, to the extent that they relate to the things of God. And none of those who are not possessed of that standard are in a position to judge him.

But the natural man does not accept the teaching of the spirit of God, for to him it is folly, and he cannot understand it, because it is subject only to spiritual tests. But the spiritual man trieth all things, yet himself is to be put on trial by none. For

Who hath understood the mind of the Lord,
And who shall give him knowledge ?

But for our part we have the mind of Christ. [1 Cor. ii. 14–16.]

There is no other foundation but Christ. He who, even though accepting that foundation, builds thereon a superstructure of human wisdom, will doubtless be saved, but as though through fire if this wisdom be of straw. Out of all that he has built, only the foundation will remain. Since a man regenerated by grace is a temple of God, the wisdom toward which he should tend is that which the Spirit of God Himself erects on an unshakable foundation—that wisdom which is folly for the world, as the wisdom of the world is folly before God.

Foundation can no man lay other than that which is laid, which is Jesus Christ. But if a man buildeth upon the foundation whether it be gold, silver, precious stones, wood, grass or straw—the work of each man shall become manifest. For the Day shall declare it, because that day is to be disclosed in fire, and the worth of each man's work shall that fire assay. If any man's work abide, which he hath built thereupon, he shall receive reward : if any man's work be burnt up, he shall lose his reward, but himself shall be saved, yet as one that hath passed through fire.

Know ye not that ye are the temple of God, and that the Spirit of God dwelleth in you ? If any man destroyeth the temple of God, him shall God destroy ; for the temple of God is holy, which temple yourselves are.

Let no man deceive himself. If any man thinketh himself wise among you in this age, let him become a fool, that he may become really wise. For the wisdom of this world is folly before God. For it is written,

He catcheth the wise in their own craftiness ; [1]

and again,

The Lord knoweth the reasonings of the wise, how fruitless they are.[2]

Wherefore let no one make boast among men. For all things are yours, whether Paul or Apollos or Cephas, whether the world or life or death, whether the present or the future—all are yours, and you are Christ's, and Christ is God's. [1 Cor. iii. 11-23.]

---

[1] Job v. 13.   [2] Ps. xciv. (xciii.) 11.

CHAPTER III

THE LAW AND GRACE

THE TEACHING OF SAINT PAUL ON THE LAW AND GRACE WAS rapidly summarized in the introduction to this book. The texts which are gathered together in this chapter will permit the reader to follow at closer range the apostle's train of argument and enter more deeply into his thought. They are chiefly drawn from the Epistle to the Romans, where the matter is formally treated.

All Will Be Judged

It is in Paul's eyes a premise beyond doubting—and pre-supposed by everything he says—that each will be judged according to his works.

Wherefore thou art without excuse, O man, whosoever thou be that judgest. In judging others thou dost condemn thyself; for thou, who art judging, art guilty of the very same misdeeds. And we know that God's condemnation of them who do such things is according to truth. Thinkest thou, O man, that judgest them who do such things yet thyself dost them, that thou wilt escape the condemnation of God? Or dost thou despise the riches of his goodness and of his forbear-ance and of his patience, not understanding that the goodness of God is to lead thee to repentance?

Yea, in the stubbornness of thine impenitent heart thou art laying up for thyself wrath on the day of wrath, of the manifestation of the just judging of God, who " will render to every man according to his works." [1] To those who by perseverance in good works are seeking after glory and honour and immortality he will render everlasting life; but for those who are factious, who disobey the truth but obey wickedness, there will be wrath and fury. [Rom. ii. 1-8.]

---

[1] Prov. xxiv. 12 ; Ps. lxii. (lxi.) 12.

He writes to the same effect in his first Epistle to the Corinthians :

Is it that ye know not that the unjust shall not inherit the kingdom of God ?
Be not deceived ; neither fornicators nor idolaters nor adulterers nor effeminates nor sodomites nor thieves nor cheats, nor drunkards nor railers, nor robbers shall inherit the kingdom of God. [1 Cor. vi. 9–10.]
He that dealeth wrongfully shall reap the fruit of his wrongdoing. [Colos. iii. 25.]

And this law is retribution for things done by Him Who "searches the reins and the hearts" is an absolutely universal law, valid for Greek as well as for Jew.

Affliction and anguish upon every human being that worketh evil, upon Jew first, and then upon Greek ; but glory and honour and peace to everyone that worketh good, to Jew first, and then to Greek. With God there is no respect of persons. [Rom. ii. 9–11.]

The pagans will be judged in accordance with their law, which is the norm of action invisibly dwelling in their conscience by virtue of nature and by virtue of the secret inspirations of God. The Jews will be judged according to their Law, which is the Law of God written and publicly manifested, the Law of Moses.

Such then as have sinned not being under the Law will perish without reference to the Law ; and such as have sinned under the Law will be punished with reference to the Law. For it is not the hearers of the Law that are just in God's sight, but it is the doers of the Law that will be justified, in the day on which, as my gospel teacheth, God will judge the secrets of man through Christ Jesus. For when the gentiles, who by nature have not the Law, fulfil the requirements of the Law, these, though they have not the Law, are a law unto themselves, showing as they do the demands of the Law to be written in their hearts ; and an approving conscience beareth them out, amid the debate of thoughts that accuse or defend. [Rom. ii. 12–15.]
Circumcision, indeed, profiteth, if thou be a doer of the Law ; but if thou be a transgressor of the Law, thy circumcision is become uncircumcision. If therefore the uncircumcised obey the commands of the Law, will not their uncircumcision be reckoned circumcision ? And then the physically uncircumcised, fulfilling the Law, shall judge thee, who with the letter thereof and the circumcision art a transgressor of the Law. [Rom. ii. 25–27.]

All are Sinners

But at once there rises before Paul's eye a tragic fact : all, Jews and Gentiles, all are sinners, and therefore condemned by their own law.

Paul does not mean to say that, if one considers individually this one and that one, there is no man who does good, be it among the Jews or among the Gentiles (he has just explicitly said the contrary). He relies rather upon a summing up of evidence, the general behaviour of Jews and pagans. And what strikes them in this summing up, taken as an outward sign of a deeper reality and of an essential truth, is the fact that every man, Jew or pagan, according as he places his confidence in himself (in the "old man" or in the "natural man") and in the law (the natural law or the Mosaic Law) in order to achieve goodness through his own effort alone, stumbles over the law and leans toward evil.

In place of the justice they sought, the Jew and the Pharisee find transgression. In place of the wisdom they sought, the Greek and the philosopher find foolishness.

In the things of nature and of the world, we find our way out by ourselves (with the ordinary help which God gives to the birds and to the grasses of the fields as he does to men). In the things of eternal life, where it is a question of entering into the divine life itself, this is not the case. It is God Who finds a way out for us, by refashioning or regenerating our being (in giving us grace) through the strength of Christ, to Whom the gift of living faith makes us vitally adhere. The basic illusion in all this is to believe that we save ourselves —or that we make ourselves just through ourselves—by the mere forces of our nature and of our will, when applied to making our conduct conform exactly to the moral rules and the religious observances externally set up before us. And this illusion is therefore to wish to reach a condition wherein we shall be sure of our own justice and goodness (because we shall have determined the fact that our conduct is indeed conformable to those rules and those observances), and wherein we shall be settled in a security before God which is based upon ourselves.

It is this basic double illusion which Paul tirelessly excoriates. And it is first and before all else among the Jews that he excoriates it, it is first and before all else against the Jews that he directs his polemics, because, unlike the Gentiles, the Jews have been chosen to watch over the things of salvation and the eternal life (" Salvation is from the Jews " [1]) and have been placed under the regimen of the written Law, explicitly formulated and publicly proclaimed, which they have received from God. And also because many among them imagined that to have received the Law and to have practised its most external observances (most external, hence the easiest for a weak humanity) sufficed for their salvation and made them certain of salvation.   And again because, now that the Messiah is come, the man of sorrows as foretold by Isaiah, Who has taken upon Himself our ailments, the Jewish illusion that no man can save himself by the works of the Law became a major obstacle to the economy of salvation, and stood in opposition to God Himself ; for not only did it turn the Jews themselves away from true salvation, but it threatened to prevent salvation and the work of God from spreading freely among all the nations of the earth by trying to subject to the ceremonial observances of the Jewish Law all those who would be believers in Jesus.

Hence the Gentiles, who attempted to arrive by themselves (and not by faith in a saving God) at the fulness of natural wisdom by virtue of the workings of their reason—as though the reason could, without that faith, arrive at its own fulness, its own perfect accomplishment—are imprisoned under sin and condemned by their own law, which is the law of the human conscience.

For the wrath of God is revealed from heaven against all impiety and wickedness of men, of such as in wickedness are repressing the truth ; because what is known about God is clear to them, for God himself hath made it clear.   For since the creation of the world his invisible attributes—his everlasting power and divinity—are to be discerned and contemplated through his works, so that they are without

---

[1] John iv. 22.

excuse, inasmuch as having come to know God, they yet have not glorified him as God or rendered thanks, but they have become vain in their reasonings, and their senseless heart was darkened. Proclaiming themselves wise, they are become fools, and they have changed the glory of the incorruptible God for the likeness of images of corruptible man, and of birds, and of beasts, and of reptiles.

Wherefore God hath delivered them over through the lusts of their hearts to uncleanness, and the dishonouring of their own bodies, because they have abandoned the truth about God for a lie, and have served and worshipped the creature in place of the Creator, who is blessed for ever, Amen.

Wherefore, I say, God hath delivered them over to shameful passions. For their women have abandoned the natural use of their bodies for the unnatural, while the men in like manner, leaving the natural use of women, have blazed with passion one for another, men perpetrating shame upon men, and incurring thereby in their own persons the meet reward of their madness.

And inasmuch as they have resolved against possessing the knowledge of God, God hath delivered them over to a reprobate mind, that they should do what is disgraceful, being filled with all wickedness, villainy, covetousness, malice ; replete with envy, murder, strife, guile, spite ; backbiters, slanderers, God-haters, insolent, arrogant, braggarts, devisers of evil, rebellious to parents, without understanding, without honour, without affection, without pity. For, realizing though they do the judgment of God—that they who do such things are worthy of death—they are not only guilty thereof themselves, but even applaud others who practise them. [Rom. i. 18–32.]

And the Jews, who attempted to arrive by themselves (and not by faith in the promised Saviour, Whose name is now known to them) at external life in virtue of the works of the Law—as though the works of the Law, and especially its first commandment, which is to love God above all things, could, without that faith, be truly accomplished in their integrity— are also imprisoned under sin and condemned by their own Law, which is the Law of God received from Angels by the hand of Moses.

But if thou bear the name of "Jew," and dost rely upon the Law, and dost make a boast of God, and dost understand his will, and dost approve the things that are more excellent, having been instructed from the Law, yea, and art confident that thou art a guide to the

blind, a light to those in darkness, an instructor of the foolish, a teacher
of the simple, since thou hast in the Law the standard of knowledge
and truth—thou, then, that teachest thy fellow, dost thou not teach
thyself? Thou that preachest against stealing—dost thou steal? Thou
that forbiddest adultery—dost thou commit adultery? Thou that
loathest idols—dost thou plunder temples? Thou that dost make a
boast of the Law—dost thou dishonour God by thy transgression
of the Law? For " the name of God," as it is written, " is blasphemed
among the gentiles because of you." [1]   [Rom. ii. 17-24.]

Jews and Gentiles, Paul bears witness against them all :

We have laid it to the charge both of Jew and Greeks that *all* are
under the power of sin, even as it is written :
There is none just, not even one,
     there is none that understandeth, there is none that seeketh out
     God ;
All have gone astray, they are become unprofitable together,
     there is none that doth goodness, there is not so much as one. [2]
     [Rom. iii. 9-12.]

Infelix homo

There is no one who is just, if we take into account that
which he can do by himself, and the embers of concupiscence
which dwell in each man's heart. Let each of us take off our
masks and know himself in truth : he knows well that he is a
sinner. When the eye of our conscience looks upon that in
us which springs from us alone, we recognize the " old man,"
the " natural man," who endures ever within the regenerated
man—at least as far as tendencies and instincts are concerned,
and on occasion as far as those impure storms which seem to
flood everything, but which do not constitute sin itself so long
as free will does not give them its seal and approval. And in
the portrait that Paul has limned we recognize ourselves.

We know that the Law is spiritual ; but I am carnal, sold into the
power of sin. For I understand not mine own actions : what I wish

---

[1] Isa. liii. 5.   Saint Paul follows the Septuagint in adding " among the Gentiles"
and " because of you."   Cf. Matt. xxiii. 15.   " Woe unto you, Scribes and
hypocrites Pharisees ! For ye compass sea and land to make one proselyte ; and
when he is become so, ye make him twofold more a son of hell than ourselves."
[2] Cf. Ps. v. x. (ix.) ; xiv. (xiii.) ; xxxvi. (xxxv.) ; cxl. (cxxxix.) ; Isa. lix.

I perform not, but what I hate I do. Now if what I do is contrary to my wish, I am admitting that the Law is excellent. In fact, it is no longer I that act, but sin dwelling within me. For I know that there dwelleth not in me, that is, in my flesh, what is good ; to wish is within my reach, but to accomplish what is excellent, no. I do not the good that I wish ; but the evil that I do not wish, that I perform. Now if I do what I wish not, it is no longer I that act, but sin dwelling within me. I find, then, this law when I wish to do what is excellent, namely, that what is evil lieth to my hand. I delight in the law of God after the inward man, but I behold another law in my members, warring against the law of my mind, and making me captive to the law of sin which is in my members.

Unhappy man that I am ! Who will deliver me from the body of this death ? Thanks be to God through our Lord Jesus Christ ! So then, one and the same self, with my mind I serve the law of God, but with my flesh the law of sin. [Rom. vii. 14-25.]

Justification by Faith

Sinners as we are, we can then be set free ; not by the power of our works, but by the power of grace which, through living faith, makes of us a new creature—a creature not only forgiven, but now made straight and just itself, because it receives its new life from the Just Man who has given satisfaction for that creature to the justice of God. The creature retains within it the embers of sin, but it is no longer a slave of sin ; it now has within it, by reason of its life in Christ, that justness which is not " from the Law," but " which is through faith in Christ " and " which cometh from God, based upon faith—that so I may know him : what the power of his resurrection, what fellowship in his sufferings ; and become one with him in his death, in the hope that I may attain to the resurrection from the dead " [Philip. iii. 9-10]. And it is God who undertakes all this ; he has called us " in virtue of his own purpose."

Ourselves also were formerly senseless, disobedient, misled, enslaved to manifold lusts and pleasures, passing our lives in malice and envy, hateful ourselves and hating one another. But when God our Saviour manifested his kindness and his love for man, he saved us, not in virtue of works of justness done by us, but out of his mercy, with the bath of regeneration and with renewal by the Holy Spirit, whom he poured out on us richly through Jesus Christ our Saviour, in order that justified by his grace we might become in hope heirs of everlasting life. [Tit. iii. 3–7.]

He it is that hath saved us and called us with a holy call, not in virtue of our works, but in virtue of his own purpose, and of the grace given us in Christ Jesus before times everlasting,[1] but now manifested by the appearing of our Saviour Jesus Christ, who hath abolished death, but hath brought life and immortality to light through the gospel. [2 Tim. i. 9–10.]

But now the justness of God hath been manifested quite apart from the Law, though witnessed to by the Law and the prophets—the justness of God through faith in Jesus Christ, for all who believe. There is no distinction ; all have sinned, and need the glory of God. By his grace they are justified freely, through the redemption which is in Christ Jesus ; whom God hath set forth a propitiation by his blood, to have effect through faith, unto the showing forth of his justness, for through the patience of God the sins of times gone by are to be passed over—unto the showing forth of his justness at the present time : so that, just himself, he will also justify him that is of faith in Jesus.

What, then, of boasting ? It is excluded. By what manner of law ? A law of works ? Nay, but by a law of faith. We reckon therefore than a man is justified by faith, quite apart from the works of the Law. Or is God the God of the Jews alone ? Is he not the God of the gentiles also ? Yea, of the gentiles also, seeing that it is one and the same God who will justify the circumcised in virtue of faith, and the uncircumcised through the same faith. Are we then making void the Law through faith ? Heaven forbid ! We are establishing the Law. [Rom. iii. 21–31.]

It is indeed the Law itself which asserts that Abraham has been established in his holiness as " father of many nations " by virtue of his faith, while yet uncircumcised (circumcision being only a sign of the alliance entered into at that moment between God and Abraham's seed in the flesh). We are justified by faith because it is the same thing for grace to cleanse us of our faults, through the power of Christ's death, and to cause us to participate in the divine life through the power of His resurrection. And also because the first act, the initial act

[1] Cf. Ephes. i. 3–14.

of this life within us is the act by which we freely open our minds to the truth of the word of God and deliver ourselves with love to the God of salvation—in other words, the act of faith, gushing into charity, the act of living faith. The justice received through faith, not being the fruit of our works, is not a good which belongs to us by right of proprietorship. It is a justice bestowed, continuously bestowed, a flowering within us of the life of Christ, a vitalizing by His blood. This justice is ours, but we no longer are our own, we have become members of Another. The doctrine of justification by faith is inseparable in Paul's thought from the doctrine of incorporation in Christ.

And now all the moral precepts of the Law, far from being destroyed, are confirmed, because Faith makes it possible to fulfil them in a lasting and complete fashion, and because from henceforth they represent only that behaviour which is fitting to a being already made just and free of sin in his root powers, to the extent that he clings to Christ and receives his life from Him. The meaning of these precepts has thus been transfigured : they no longer command bad men to be good and to grow into something which they are not ; rather do they command good men not to be bad, and not to fail in that which they already are, not to fall back into the state of slavery from whence they have been freed. Justification is received through faith, quite apart from works. But once justified, man is more than ever held to good works (be it only, as it was in the case of the good thief, as far as the disposition of the soul is concerned). And this is not because the works of man would have power to save man by themselves, but because good works proceed from the charity which has been given to man and which is his life—his new and eternal life—and which is joined to faith when faith is living : " faith working through charity " [Gal. v. 6]. And also because the works of charity, which is a fruitful and effective life, themselves are deserving of life, to the extent that man, acting freely under the inflowing of grace, receives from God's mercy the dignity of being a cause — secondary and instrumental — in the matter of his salvation. " God is not unjust so as to forget your works . . ." [Heb. vi. 10]. ". . . The crown of justness which the Lord, the just judge, shall award to me on that day " [2 Tim. iv. 8].

Concerning this necessity of good works, Paul clearly explains himself to the Corinthians, of whom several had misunderstood his doctrine, and seemed to understand the freedom he preached as a freedom to do anything.

Be not deceived ; neither fornicators nor idolaters nor adulterers nor effeminates nor sodomites nor thieves nor cheats, nor drunkards, nor railers, nor robbers shall inherit the kingdom of God. And such some of you were ; but yet ye have washed yourselves clean, but ye have been hallowed, but ye have been justified in the name of the Lord Jesus Christ and in the Spirit of our God.

" All things are lawful to me "—but not all things are profitable. " All things are lawful to me "—but to nothing will I become enslaved. . . .

Know ye not that your bodies are members of Christ ? Am I then to take the members of Christ and make them members of a harlot ? God forbid ! Or know ye not that he that cleaveth to a harlot is one body with her ? " The two," it is said, " shall become one flesh." But he that cleaveth to the Lord is one spirit with him. Flee from impurity. Every other sin that a man committeth is a thing outside the body ; but the impure sinneth against his own body. Know ye not that your body is the temple of the Holy Spirit who is within you, whom ye have from God ? And ye are not your own, for ye have been bought at a price. Glorify God, then, in your body. [1 Cor. vi. 9–12 ; 15–20.]

And in like fashion he writes :

Seeing that we have died to sin, how can we live any longer therein ? Know ye not, that as many of us as were baptized unto Christ Jesus, we were baptized unto his death ? We were buried therefore with him through this baptism unto death, that as Christ was raised from the dead through the glory of the Father, so we also should walk in newness of life. For if we have become one with him in likeness of his death, why, then, we shall also be in likeness of his resurrection. For this we know, that our old man hath been crucified with him, in order that our sinful body may be brought to naught, and ourselves no longer be slaves to sin ; for he that hath died is acquitted of sin. Now if we died with Christ, we believe that we shall also live with him, knowing as we do that Christ, raised from the dead, dieth no more, death no more hath power over him. His death he died to sin, once and for all ;

his life he liveth to God. Even thus do ye reckon yourselves to be dead to sin, but living to God in Christ Jesus.

Let not sin, then, reign in your mortal body, so that ye obey the lusts thereof, neither offer ye your members as tools of wickedness to sin ; but offer yourselves to God as men come to life from the dead, and your members to God as tools of justness. For sin shall not have power over you, since ye are not under the Law, but under grace. [Rom. vi. 2–14.]

Jesus gave himself for us in order that he might . . . purify a people to be peculiarly his own, zealous for good works. [Tit. ii. 14.]

We are saved by grace, through faith, and that not of ourselves . . . [and] created in Christ Jesus for good works, which God hath prepared beforehand that therein we may walk. [Ephes. ii. 8–10.]

The Just Man Lives of Faith and of Charity

I am not ashamed of the gospel ; for it is the power of God bringing salvation to every one that believeth, to Jew first, and then to Greek. For the justness of God is revealed therein, leading men from faith unto faith, according as it is written, " The just man shall live by faith." [1]—[Rom. i. 16–17.]

Even though he feels ever within him the workings of sin (but from thenceforth he is no longer subject thereto ; he is stronger than it), the just man lives from a divine life, which is not a life according to the flesh either, and which makes him in truth an adopted son of God.

Our commonwealth (πολίτευμα, citizenship) is in the heavens. [Philip. iii. 20.]

There is now no condemnation, therefore, for those in Christ Jesus. For the law of the Spirit of the life in Christ Jesus hath delivered thee from the law of sin and death. The powerlessness of the Law, the weakness thereof through the flesh, God hath made good ; sending his own Son in the likeness of sinful flesh and as a sin-offering, he hath condemned sin in the flesh, in order that the demands of the Law may be fulfilled in us, who walk not according to the flesh but according to the spirit. For they that are according to the flesh mind the things of the flesh, but they that are according to the spirit, the things of the spirit. Now the mind of the flesh is death, but the mind of the

---

[1] Hab. i. 4 (lxx.).

spirit life and peace ; because the mind of the flesh is enmity towards God, for it is not subject to the law of God, neither can it be. And they that are in the flesh cannot please God.

Now ye are not in the flesh but in the spirit, seeing that the Spirit of God dwelleth within you. But if any man hath not the Spirit of Christ, that man is not of Christ. And if Christ be in you, your body is dead by reason of sin, but your spirit is life by reason of justness. And if the Spirit of him who raised Jesus from the dead dwelleth within you, then he who raised Christ Jesus from the dead will also bring to life your mortal bodies through his Spirit who dwelleth within you.

So, then, brethren, we are debtors, not to the flesh, that we should live according to the flesh—for if ye live according to the flesh, ye shall surely die ; but if by the spirit ye do to death the practices of the body, ye shall live. For as many as are led by the Spirit of God, these are the sons of God. For ye have not received the spirit of slavery, to be once more in fear, but ye have received the spirit of adoption, whereby we cry, " Abba ! Father ! " The Spirit himself beareth witness with our spirit that we are the children of God. And if children, heirs also : heirs of God, and joint-heirs with Christ—if, that is, we suffer with him, that with him we may also be glorified.

For I reckon that the sufferings of the present time are not worthy to be compared with the glory to be revealed in us. Yea, creation with eager straining awaiteth the manifestation of the children of God. For creation was made subject to vanity—not of its own will, but by reason of him who subjected it—yet with hope that creation itself shall be freed from its slavery to corruption unto the freedom of the glory of the children of God. For we know that all creation doth groan and travail together to this hour. And not only so, but ourselves, too, who have the firstfruits of the Spirit—we ourselves groan within ourselves while awaiting adoption, the redemption of our body. For in hope were we saved : and hope beheld is not hope : for how can a man hope for what he beholdeth ? But if we hope for what we behold not, we await it in patience.

And in like manner the Spirit also beareth up our weakness. For we know not how we are to pray as we ought ; but the Spirit himself pleadeth in our behalf with unutterable groanings. And he who searcheth hearts knoweth what is the mind of the Spirit, how he pleadeth before God in behalf of the saints.

And we know that to them that love God all things work together unto good, for them that are the called according to his purpose. For those whom he hath foreknown, them he hath predestined to bear a nature in the image of his Son's, that he should be first-born among many brethren. And those whom he hath predestined, them he hath also called : and those whom he hath called, them he hath also justified : and those whom he hath justified, them he hath also glorified.

Well, then, what are we to say ? If God is for us, who shall be against us ? Seeing that he hath not spared his own Son, but hath delivered him for all of us, how can he fail to grant us all things with him ? Who shall lay charge against the elect of God ? " It is God who justifieth ; who is to condemn ? " [1] It is Christ Jesus who died, or rather was raised from the dead, he who is at the right hand of God, who also pleadeth in our behalf.

Who shall separate us from the love of Christ ? Shall affliction or anguish or persecution or hunger or nakedness or danger or the sword ? Even as it is written,

> For thy sake we suffer death all the day long
> we are regarded as sheep for the slaughter.[2]

Yet amidst all this we more than conquer through him who hath loved us. For I am confident that neither death, nor life, nor angels, nor principalities, nor things present, nor things to come, nor powers, nor height, nor depth, nor any other creature shall be able to separate us from the love of God in Christ Jesus our Lord. [Rom. viii. 1-39.]

The just man is saved in hope. He knows that all things work together for the good of those who love God. He knows that if he does not himself voluntarily strip off God's eternal love made manifest in Christ, nothing will be able to separate him from that love. He knows that God first loved him, and that He Who so loved him that He willed to die for his faults has a love faithful enough and strong enough to lift him up when he falls and help him to the end. The just man's confidence in Him in Whom he has faith is more sure than any evidence. Christian hope, which detaches the soul from every sensible sign and from all human support, is more sure than any acquired security and more sure than the physical evidence —for which the Jews yearned—of having fulfilled the works of the Law. Even as the illusion of making oneself just before God by oneself and by one's works has been replaced by the knowledge of justification by faith in Another than oneself,

[1] Isa. l. 8-9.   [2] Ps. xliv. (xliii.) 22.

5

so also the illusion that one could come to be sure of one's own justice, by being assured that one has exactly fulfilled all the works of the Law, is replaced by the knowledge of the redeeming love of Another and by confidence in that love. The just man lives by faith ; that applies to all his spiritual life, and even to the pains he is at to please God. Paul brings insecurity up to the very heart of the spiritual life, only to over-come it by the confidence of faith. " I know naught against myself, yet I am not thereby acquitted, but he that trieth me is the Lord " [1 Cor. iv. 4]. The just man knows that he loves God ; he does not know whether he loves Him enough to be saved. He lives by faith : he no longer needs to know any-thing. He builds his whole life on the firm confidence that he is reconciled, but that confidence does not come to him from a " scientific " certainty which relates to the observances fulfilled by him ; rather it comes to him from the certainty of the faith which relates to Christ and to His love, not to himself and to his condition before God. This confidence grounded in faith is the certainty of hope. To her judges who treacherously asked her whether she was in a state of grace, Jeanne d'Arc replied : " If I am, God keep me so ; if I am not, God make me so."

Justified therefore by faith, let us have peace with God through our Lord Jesus Christ, through whom we have obtained our access by faith into this grace wherein we stand and exult in the hope of the glory of God. And not only so, but we exult in our tribulations also, knowing that tribulation worketh endurance, and endurance experience, and experience hope. And hope doth not prove false, for the charity of God [the love of God for us] is poured forth in our hearts through the Holy Spirit who hath been given us, so surely as Christ, while we were yet weak, died in due season, on behalf of the impious.

For scarcely will any one die on behalf of a just man—for a good man perhaps some one might even dare to die — but God proveth his charity towards us in that while we were yet sinners Christ died in our behalf. All the more therefore, now that we are justified by his blood, shall we be saved through him from the wrath. For if when we were enemies we were reconciled to God through the death of his Son, all the more, once reconciled, shall we be saved by his life. And not only so, but we exult in God through our Lord Jesus Christ, through whom we have even now received this reconciliation. [Rom. v. 1-11.]

Thus all Saint Paul's teaching implies a return toward the inward and the spiritual. The life of the soul is no longer centred in the visible—on works and on the Law—but on the invisible, and on that eminently invisible thing, the mystery of God in us. As I pointed out in my introductory pages, here is a characteristic effect of the spiritual revolution wrought by the Gospel. That which is primary in the New Law, and that in which reside all its power, is not a written code nor outward observances, but the grace of the Holy Spirit dwelling in those who believe. Because it is in agreement with the condition of being human and with the fundamental law of the Incarnation, Christianity gives—and must give—an essential place to that which is visible and outwardly manifest, but it is nevertheless true that the hidden and the inward matters more to it than the outward and the apparent. And to the extent that Christianity ceases recognizing this primacy of the invisible over the visible, to that extent Christian life withers, risks drying up. Not observances and practices, but faith and love and interior purity—the circumcision of the heart—make the Christian, the true Israelite according to the spirit. *In abscondito Judaeus.*

For he is not a Jew who is one outwardly, neither is that circumcision which is outward, in the flesh. He is a Jew who is inwardly so, and that is circumcision which is of the heart, in the spirit, not in the letter; the praise whereof is not from men but from God. [Rom. ii. 28-29.]

The Law is Holy and Bears with it Death

The Law is holy because it is the created expression of the wisdom of God. But while the Law makes us know evil, it does not give us the strength to avoid evil. And by making evil known, the Law is, for evil, an occasion for tempting us; and the wages of evil is death. [Rom. vi. 23.] Thus the Law

bears death with it.   If there were no law, there would be no
transgression, and hence there would be no death.[1]   This is
true, in a sense, concerning the moral law generally ;   suppose
the impossible, that such a law were not impressed in our hearts ;
then there could be no transgression and hence no punishment.
But all this is especially true of the Law promulgated on
Sinai, and it is to this Law that what Paul says applies directly
and above all.   The Mosaic Law casts upon the conscience,
with divine authority, a light which we cannot put aside,
much more piercing and more implacable than the natural
light cast by our weak reason in its search after the natural
law.   And the requirements (of holiness) to which the Law
subjects men are far more rigorous, and the end (salvation)
toward which it tends much higher, than the natural happiness
and the natural duties of which pagan sages had conceived
an idea.   Paul's line of reasoning supposes this fact, that the
Jews have been set apart, in view of the world's salvation,
for a purity and holiness of life—highly superior, even though
principally external, to the moral ideals of all the gentiles—
which were required by the Law and for whose fulfilment
not the Law, but the grace of the Christ to come (and now come)
alone is efficacious.   A people elect, and a people victim—they
are bound up in their Law as though in God's trap—so long as
they rely upon the Law, not on living faith, and so long as
they withhold faith in Him Whose death, wrought by their
Priesthood in the name of the Law, now brings them their
deliverance.   But this deliverance, which implies that salvation
comes to all by the Cross, not by the Law, requires also that the
Jews recognize that the regimen of the Law has come to an
end, and that at the same time they renounce the keeping to
themselves alone of the privileges which that regimen conferred
to them.

[1] According to Saint Paul, death is the price of a transgression, not of the natural
law, but of the positive divine law. If man had been created in a state of pure
nature, death would only have been a consequence of our natural state, it would
not have come upon us as a punishment for a transgression. But man having
been created in the state of innocence, which supernaturally implied exemption
from death, it was by the breaking of the positive commandment given to Adam
that man lost this privilege, and that death for us made its appearance in the
world. (Cf. Rom. v. 12–14.)

The Law worketh wrath ; and where there is no law, neither is there transgression. [Rom. iv. 15.]

What, then, are we to say ? Is the Law sin ? Heaven forbid ! Yet I know not sin save through the Law. For indeed I had not known lust, if the Law had not said, " Thou shalt not lust " ; but sin, getting a hold on me through the commandment, worked all manner of lust in me ; for without the Law sin is dead. I was once living without the Law ; but when the commandment came, sin sprang into life, and I died, and the very commandment that was for life I found to be my death. For sin, getting a hold on me through the commandment, deceived me and killed me thereby. The Law, therefore, is holy, and the commandment holy, and just and good. Hath what is good, then, become death to me ? Heaven forbid ! But sin, that it might be seen as sin, worked death in me through what was good, in order that sin might come to be sinful beyond measure by reason of the commandment. [Rom. vii. 7–13.]

Now we know that whatsoever the Law saith is addressed to those under the Law, that every mouth may be stopped, and the whole world become accountable to God : because from the works of the Law " no flesh shall be justified before him " : for through the Law is realization of sin. [Rom. iii. 19–20.]

The sting of death is sin, and the power of sin is the Law. [I Cor. xv. 56–57.]

Thus the Law suffices to punish ; it does not suffice to save. Here is a particular case of that dissymmetry which is always found between the good, of which we are incapable without God, and the evil of which we are capable, ourselves alone. And the divine inflowing, which in vitalizing us gives us the power to act as good men (not half-heartedly, or limpingly, but lastingly and completely), is the grace of Christ and supposes (supernatural) faith in Him, because the goal toward which it makes us tend is entrance into the very joy of God and into His glory. It was by this grace of the Christ to come, and by faith in Him, that lived the just men of the Old Law, and those of the times of the Patriarchs.

Christ Frees Us of the Regimen of the Law

We are no longer held to the multitude of ceremonial precepts nor to the juridical rules of the Mosaic Law ; we are held to other ceremonial precepts less onerous and less numerous. And we are ever held to the moral precepts of the Law ; but we are held thereto as to the requirements of the very life and freedom which are within us, not as to requirements which do us violence and exceed our capacity. And because the whole law is summed up in love—in the love for our brothers *even as Christ loved them*, in the new commandment given by Christ—by the very fact the law itself becomes inward. For " as we love so is our weight," as Saint Augustine was later to say. Thus the New Law is less burdensome than the Old Law, even though it prescribes a more difficult purity and holiness. If the New Law requires many less things beyond the prescriptions of the natural law, and many less ceremonial observances than the Old Law, in return it requires that which is the most difficult of all : purity in the hidden movements and the internal acts of the soul. But love makes light the yoke of this higher perfection : a yoke too heavy for him who does not love (but he who loves not has already cut himself off from life) ; and freedom for him who loves.[1]

We are no longer " under the Law," which is to say that we are quit of the regimen of the Law, quit of that condition of humanity wherein the government of its actions had, as its basic rule, no longer the natural light and the internal promptings of conscience, as in the days of the Patriarchs, and not as yet the promulgation of the Gospel, as after Christ's coming, but the promulgation of the written Law transmitted by Moses. We have passed under the regimen of the New Law, which is a law of freedom.

Or know ye not, brethren—I am speaking to those who understand the Law—that the Law hath power over a man for such a time only as he remaineth alive ? The married woman is bound by the Law to her living husband ; but if her husband die, she is quit of the law of the husband. So, then, while her husband liveth, she will be called an adulteress if she unite herself to another man ; but if her husband die, she is free from that law, and will not be an adulteress if she unite

---

[1] Cf. Saint Augustine, *De Natura et Gratia*, c. lxii., and Saint Thomas Aquinas, *Sum. Theol.*, i.–ii. 107, 4.

herself to another man. Now ye, my brethren, have been made to die to the Law in the body of Christ, so as to belong to another, even to him who hath been raised from the dead, that we should bear fruit for God. For when we were in the flesh, the sinful passions aroused by the Law were working in our members, so that we bore fruit for death ; but we are now quit of the Law, having died to that whereby we were held down, so as to serve in newness of spirit and not in oldness of letter. [Rom. vii. 1-6.]

I died to the Law through the Law [1] in order that I might live to God. With Christ I am nailed to the cross ; it is no longer I that live, but Christ that liveth in me. So far as I live now in the flesh, I live by faith in the Son of God, who loved me and delivered himself for me. I make not void the grace of God ; for if justness is come through the Law, then Christ died for naught. [Gal. ii. 19-21.]

Even thus Abraham " believed God and it was reckoned to him justness." [2]

Know, then, that they that are of faith, they are the sons of Abraham. The Scripture foresaw that it was through faith that God would justify the gentiles and foretold to Abraham, " in thee shall all the nations be blessed." [3] And so they that are of faith are blessed with faithful Abraham. Whereas they that are of the works of the Law are under a curse, for it is written, " Accursed is every man that abideth not by all things that are written in the book of the Law, so as to do them." [4] Now, that by the Law no one is justified before God is manifest, because " the just man shall live by faith." [5] But the Law doth not rest upon faith, nay, " he that doth practise them shall live by them." [6] Christ hath ransomed us from the curse of the Law by becoming a curse on our behalf (for it is written, " accursed is every man that hangeth upon a tree "),[7] that the blessing of Abraham may come to the gentiles in Jesus Christ, that in virtue of faith we may receive the promised Spirit.

Brethren, I speak in human terms. Still, when a man's will hath been ratified, no one maketh it void or addeth thereto. Now the promises were spoken to Abraham " and to his seed." [8] It saith not, " and to his seeds," as though there were many, but as of one, " and to

---

[1] " Through the Law," because it was by virtue of the Law that Christ, having taken upon Himself my sins, suffered the death which delivered me from sin and from the regimen of the Law.

[2] Gen. xv. 6 : cf. Rom. iv., where the passage is expounded at some length.

[3] Gen. xii. 3 ; xviii. 18.   [4] Deut. xxvii. 26.

[5] Hab. ii. 4.   [6] Levit. xviii. 5.

[7] Deut. xxi .23 (lxx.).   [8] Cf. Gen. xii. 7 : etc.

his seed " ; which seed is Christ. Now this I say. The Law, which came into being four hundred and thirty years later, doth not annul the covenant already ratified by God, so as to make the promise void. For if the right to inherit be from the Law, it cannot be from a promise, whereas God made the grant to Abraham by way of a promise.

What, then, of the Law ? It was added for the sake of transgressions, until the seed should come to which the promise was made. It was commanded by angels through an intermediary. Now there is no intermediary where there is only one [where there is a mediator, there is a contract between two parties] ; but [in the promise] it is God alone [who binds himself]. Is the Law, then, at variance with the promises of God ? Heaven forbid ! If a Law had been given that was able to give life, truly justness would be from the Law. But the Scripture hath imprisoned all things under sin, that what was promised may be given in virtue of faith in Jesus Christ to them that believe.

Before the coming of faith we were in prison under the ward of the Law, waiting for the faith that was to be revealed. And so the Law has been our tutor [pedagogue] unto Christ, that we may be justified through faith. But now that faith hath come, we are no longer under the tutor. For ye are all through your faith sons of God in Christ Jesus. For all of you who were baptized into Christ, have put on Christ. In him is neither Jew nor Greek, neither slave nor free, neither male nor female ; for ye are all one person in Christ Jesus. And if ye are Christ's, then are ye the seed of Abraham, and heirs by promise. [Gal. iii. 6–29.] [1]

The pedagogue in antiquity was the slave who had charge of a child at home, and accompanied him to school. The Mosaic Law was the pedagogue who prepared us for Christ. Now that Christ is come, we are no longer under the pedagogue. We are no longer under the regimen of the Law. Those who believe in Jesus Christ are subject to the law of God, not as to a pedagogue who leads children along in spite of themselves, but as to a light along the path of freedom which man capable of leading themselves follow of their own choosing.

Now I say, as long as the heir is a child, he differeth in no way from a slave, though he is the master of all, but he is under guardians and

---

[1] See also Gal. ii. 11–16, where Paul relates how he reprimanded Peter for having refused temporarily to eat with Gentiles ; also Gal. iii. 1–5.

stewards until the day fixed by his father. So we too, when we were children, were enslaved under the elements of the world ; but when the fullness of time came, God sent forth his Son, born of a woman, born under the Law, to ransom them that were under the Law, that we might enter upon our adoption as sons. And because ye are sons, God hath sent forth the Spirit of his Son into our hearts, crying, " Abba, Father ! " Wherefore thou art no longer a slave, but a son ; and if a son ; an heir also by the act of God. [Gal. iv. 1-7.]

Tell me, ye that wish to be under the Law, will ye not listen to the Law ? For it is written that Abraham had two sons, one by the slave and one by the free. The one by the slave was begotten according to the flesh, the one by the free in virtue of the promise. Now these things befell in allegory. For these women are the two convenants, the one from Mount Sinai, bringing forth children unto slavery ; which is Hagar. For Sinai is a mountain in Arabia, and answereth to the Jerusalem that now is, for she is in slavery with her children. But the Jerusalem which is on high is free, which is our mother : for it is written,

Rejoice, thou barren one, that bringest not forth,
cry out and shout, thou that travailest not,
For many are the children of her that is desolate,
more than of her that hath a husband.[1]

Ye, brethren, are children of promise, as Isaac was. But as at that time he that was begotten according to the flesh persecuted him that was according to the spirit, so also now. But what saith the Scripture ? " Cast out the slave and her son, for the son of the slave shall not be heir with the son " [2] of the free. Hence, brethren, we are not children of a slave but of the free.

With freedom did Christ make us free ; stand fast, then, and be not caught again under the yoke of slavery.

Behold, I Paul tell you that if ye let yourselves be circumcised, Christ shall profit you nothing. Again, I protest to every man that letteth himself be circumcised, that he is bound to observe the whole of the Law. Ye are severed from Christ, all ye that would be justified by the Law, ye are fallen from grace. Whereas we in spirit by virtue of faith eagerly await the justness for which we hope. For in Christ Jesus neither circumcision nor uncircumcision availeth anything, but faith working through charity. [Gal. iv. 21-31 ; v. 1-6.]

---

[1] Isa. liv. 1.   [2] Gen. xxi. 10.

God's Plan

In one of the texts from the Epistle to the Galatians which I have just quoted, and in another from the Epistle to the Romans which will be quoted below, there are two very brief sentences which discover to us what Saint Paul held to be the most profound secret of wisdom. This secret relates to the wisdom of God.

Where sin hath been multiplied, grace hath abounded yet more. [Rom. v. 20.]

The Scripture hath imprisoned all things under sin, that what was promised may be given by virtue of faith in Jesus Christ to them who believe.   [Gal. iii. 22.] [1]

[1] Cf. Rom. xi. 32 : " God hath imprisoned all alike in disobedience, in order that he may have mercy on all."

CHAPTER IV

THE MYSTERY OF ISRAEL

S AINT PAUL'S TEACHING ON ISRAEL AND HIS TEACHING ON
the Law make up one and the same doctrine. What was
set forth in the preceding chapter is the anticipatory
commentary for this chapter.

The Tragedy of Israel

What then are we to say? Why, that the gentiles, who were not
seeking after justness, have attained justness—but the justness that is
of faith; whereas Israel, seeking after the law of justness, is not come
unto the law [of justice].

And why? Because [they have sought a justness coming not]
from faith, but from works. They have stumbled at "the stone of
stumbling," according as it is written,

Behold, I lay in Sion a stone to stumble at, and a rock to trip over;
and he that believeth in him shall not be put to shame.[1]

[Rom. ix. 30-33.]

Under the regimen of the Mosaic Law, as under the regimen
of the law of nature, which both were as the bark hiding the
secret of God, it was already (but without its being made known)
faith, faith in Him—still unknown—Who was to come, which
justified souls. Now that He is come and that He has made
Himself known, apostolic preaching everywhere announces
His name and the revelation of the Son of God. And the
barriers between Jews and gentiles fall away, because all, being
manifest and publicly called to Salvation in Him, pass under a
new regimen (the New Law) which reconciles them all in
Him. But the stubborn people, bound up in the letter of the
Law, does not understand, and wishes to remain settled in a
regimen from henceforth outworn.

Even so saith the scripture, "no one that believeth in him shall be
put to shame."[2] There is no distinction of Jew and Greek; for there

---

[1] Isa. xxviii. 6; viii. 14.　　　　[2] Isa. xxviii. 16 (lxx.).

is the same Lord of all, rich unto all that call upon him. " Whosoever shall call upon the name of the Lord shall be saved." [1]

How then are they to call upon him in whom they have not believed ? And how are they to believe in him whom they have not heard ? And how are they to hear without a preacher ? And how are men to preach unless they be sent ? As it is written, " How beautiful are the feet of them that bring glad tidings of good things ! " [2]

But not all have obeyed the gospel. For Isaiah saith, " Lord, who hath believed our report ? " [3] Therefore faith is by hearing, and hearing is through the word of Christ. But I say, have they not heard ? Why,

> Their voice hath gone forth unto all the earth,
>> and their words to the ends of the world. [4]

But again I say, hath not Israel known ? First there is Moses, who saith,

> I will rouse you to jealousy at that which is no nation,
>> and to anger at a nation void of understanding. [5]

And Isaiah declareth boldly,

> I have been found by those who sought me not,
> I have become manifest to those who enquired not of me.

But to Israel he saith,

> All the day long I have stretched out my hands
>> to a people who disobey and contradict. [6] [Rom. x. 11-21.]

Paul gives Witness to His People

If it is faith and not the Law, even under the regimen of the Law, which has already saved souls, if the true Jew is not he who is circumcised in the flesh, but he who is a Jew inwardly and by the spirit, *in abscondito Judaeus*, " where the advantage of the Jew, or what the profit of the circumcision ? "

Great in every way [replies Paul]. In the first place, they were entrusted with the oracles of God. [Rom. iii. 1-3.]

That was the first privilege of Israel. It received the deposit of the Scriptures. And if it is unfaithful, the trust confided to Israel will turn against Israel ; it will not disappear because of Israel's faithlessness ; the promises of God will be realized at Israel's expense, which will still remain, even in its misfortune, God's witness in human history : men's lack of faith " does

[1] Joel ii. 32 (iii. 5).   [2] Isa. lii. 7.   [3] Isa. liii. 1.
[4] Ps. xix. (xviii.) 4.   [5] Deut. xxxii. 21.   [6] Isa. lxv. 1-2.

not do away with the faithfulness of God." Circumcision was but the sign of Israel's election, which Israel itself disowned by not preferring circumcision to the reality which is already come, and of which circumcision was the symbol.

In expressing his love for the Jewish people, and his sorrow over them—Paul would wish to be rejected himself if that were the price of the salvation of his brothers—he enumerates the nine other prerogatives of the Jewish people : it bears the name of Israel, God's well-beloved. It is the adopted son of God. To it was made manifest the glory, the *schechina*, that supernatural brilliance in which the ark and the temple were at times enveloped. To it belong the repeated covenants entered into between God and His people. To it belong the Torah, established by the angels and published by Moses in the midst of the lightnings of Sinai. To it, the revealed worship, the messianic promises, the patriarchs. And, finally, to it, Christ, born of the lineage of Abraham and of the blood of David according to the flesh. He who is at the same time sovereign Lord of the ages.

I speak truth in Christ, I lie not, my conscience bearing me out in the Holy Spirit—I have great sorrow and unceasing grief in my heart. For I could wish to be anathema myself from Christ on behalf of my brethren, my kinsmen according to the flesh, who are Israelites, whose is the adoption and the glory and the covenants and the legislation and the liturgy and the promises, whose are the fathers, and of whom is Christ according to the flesh, who is over all, God blessed for ever, Amen. [Rom. ix. 1-5.]

Brethren, my heart's desire and my petition to God are in their behalf, for their salvation. I bear them witness that they have zeal for God, but not according to knowledge ; ignorant of the justness of God, and seeking to set up a justness of their own, they have not submitted to the justness of God. For Christ is the consummation of the Law, so that justness is for every one that believeth. [Rom. x. 1-4.]

God has not cast off His People, but Israel's Lapse is the Salvation of the Nations

I say therefore, hath " God cast off his people ? " [1] Heaven forbid! For I too am an Israelite of the seed of Abraham, of the tribe of Benjamin.

---

[1] I Sam. (I Kings) xii. 22 ; Ps. xciv. (xciii.) 14.

" God hath not cast off his people," whom he foreknew. Or know ye
not what the scripture saith in the story of Elias—how he accuseth
Israel before God ? " Lord, they have slain thy prophets, they have
overthrown thine altars ; I alone am left, and they are seeking my
life ! "[1] But what is the divine answer ? " I have left myself seven
thousand men who have not bent the knee to Baal."[2] In the same way,
therefore, at the present time there hath also come to be a remnant,
selected out of grace ; and if it is by grace, it is no more in virtue of
works, else grace were grace no more.

What then shall we say ? What Israel is seeking after, this it hath
not attained ; yet the election hath attained it. But the rest hath been
hardened, as it is written, " God hath given them a spirit of stupor,
eyes that are not to see, and ears that are not to hear, as unto this very
day."[3] And David saith :

> Let their table become a snare and a trap to them,
>   a stumbling-block and a retribution ;
> Let their eyes be darkened that they see not,
>   and bend their backs for ever down ![4]   [Rom. xi. 1-10.]

As the context clearly shows, Paul is not here thinking of a
hardening, with regard to eternal life, of Jews taken individually
who remain bound to the Mosaic Law (like other non-Chris-
tians, they can be in a state of grace if they are in good faith :
that is God's secret). He is thinking of the hardening of the
people, taken collectively, with regard to its vocation.

I say, then, have they stumbled to their fall ? Heaven forbid !
But by their lapse salvation is come to the gentiles that the latter may
" rouse them to jealousy."[5] And if their misstep is the riches of the
world, and their diminution the riches of the gentiles, how much more
their fulness ?   [Rom. xi. 11-12.]

" It is not possible to express the prerogative of Israel more
forcibly than in this verse of an epistle which, let us not forget,
is addressed to the Romans. To the extent that the misstep
of the chosen people reveals itself as a riches ! Riches for the
cosmos, riches for the pagan world. . . . Their conversion
will have a meaning greater still than their lapse, for the cosmos
and for the gentiles."[6]

[1] I (III) Kings xix. 10.   [2] I (III) Kings xix. 18.
[3] Isa. xxix. 10 ; Deut. xxix. 4.   [4] Ps. lxix. (lxviii.) 22-23 (lxx.) etc.
[5] Deut. xxxii. 21.
[6] Eric Peterson, Le Mystère des Juifs et des Gentils dans l'Eglise, pp. 56-7.

" By their lapse salvation has come to the gentiles." Here is, as Father Lagrange points out, " a statement of fact. Paul, seeing himself repulsed by the Jews, turned toward the gentiles [Acts xiii. 45-48] who therefore were earlier put in the way of salvation." [1] Moreover, and more profoundly, it must be granted that it was due to the incredulity of the Jews that the Church was able from its birth to rise up as independent of Israel taken according to the flesh, of its temporal destinies and of its theocracy, and to appear to the world with a character of absolute, supra-temporal and supra-national, universality.

" If the Jews," continues Father Legrange, " had become converts as a whole, would they have agreed to relinquish their Law ? Would Christianity have become that religion, independent of national observances, which alone could suit the gentiles ? The learned of to-day agree perfectly with Paul in asserting that the refusal of the Jews made easier the entrance of the gentiles. And even in this, God was planning the salvation of the Jews ; He wished to make them jealous, etc." [2]

" And if their misstep is the riches of the world, and their diminution the riches of the gentiles, how much more their fulness ! " " If their dispossession hath been the reconciliation of the world, what will their reintegration be but life from the dead ? " [Rom. xi. 12 ; 15.]

" Their spiritual abundance, or their multitude converted to God," wrote Saint Thomas Aquinas, " will make the riches of the gentiles, according to the saying of Ecclesiastes : *my dwelling is in the fullness of the saints.* And thus if God for the benefit of the whole world has permitted the misstep and the dispossession of the Jews, how much more generously will He restore their ruins for the advantage of the whole world. . . . And what will be the effect of their reintegration, if not to call back to life the gentiles, that is to say the lukewarm faithful, when ' on account of the progress of iniquity, the charity of a great number shall have waxed cold ' [Matt. xxiv. 12] ? " [3]

The writers of the Middle Ages saw in the reintegration of Israel the characteristic sign of the third age of the Church

[1] Lagrange, *Epitre aux Romains.*   [2] *Ibid.*
[3] Saint Thomas Aquinas, *Comm. in ep. ad Romanos*, c. xi., lect. 2.

and of Christianity.[1] Bossuet writes in the same temper :
" The Saviour Whom Sion did not recognize and Whom the
children of Jacob rejected, will turn toward them, will wipe
away their sins and will restore to them that understanding
of the prophecies which they will long have lost, in order that
it may ever be passed in succession from hand to hand unto all
posterity and be never again forgot until the end of the world,
and for as long a time as it shall please God that the world
shall endure after this marvellous event." [2] For we have the
right to believe that " it will not be with the end of the world,
but rather with the most astonishing splendour of the world,
that the conversion of the Jews will coincide." [3]

The Gentiles are Grafted upon the Olive Tree of Israel

I speak now to you gentiles. So far as I am an apostle of the gentiles,
I glorify my ministry, in the hope that I may " rouse " those of mine
own flesh " to jealousy " and save some of them. For if their dispossession hath been the reconciliation of the world, what will the
reintegration of them be but life from the dead ?

If the first fruit of the dough is holy, so is the whole mass ; and if
the root is holy, so are the branches. Now if some of the branches
have been broken off, and thou, being a wild olive, hast been ingrafted
among them, and hast become a partaker with them of the root, in
the fatness of the olive tree, boast not over those branches. And if thou
do boast, still it is not thou that upholdest the root, but the root thee.

Thou wilt say, therefore, " Branches were broken off, in order that
I might be grafted in." True : they were broken off because of their
lack of faith, and it is because of thy faith that thou dost stand. Be
not proud-minded, but fear ; for if God hath not spared the natural
branches, neither will he spare thee. [Rom. xi. 13-21.]

---

[1] Cf. the second commentary on the *Song of Songs*, attributed to Thomas
Aquinas.

[2] Bossuet, *Histoire Universelle*, 2nd part, chap. 20.

[3] Abbé Lémann, *La Question du Messie*, p. 150. Father Allo thinks that the
conversion of Israel will take place rather before than after the appearance of the
" man of sin." It seems to me in better conformity with the body of eschato-
logical scriptural texts that this should coincide with the defeat and destruction
of the Antichrist. Saint Augustine grants that between the annihilation of the
Antichrist and the end of the world there will be an interval. This will doubtless
be a long period of time, says Father Zucconi in his commentary on the
Apocalypse. Cf. Father Fortuné de la Vallette, *Apocalypse de St. Jean*, in Revue
de l'Université d'Ottawa, July–September, 1938, to April–June, 1939.

This ingrafting of the gentiles is no less great a mystery ; it is the complement of the mystery of the lapse of Israel.

Wherefore remember that aforetime ye, the gentiles according to the flesh—ye that are styled " uncircumcision " by that which is styled " circumcision," a circumcision done with hands in the flesh —remember that ye were at that time Christless, alienated from the commonwealth of Israel and strangers to the covenants of the promise, without hope and without God in the world. But now in Christ Jesus ye that were once far off are brought near through the blood of Christ.

For he is our peace, he that hath made both one, and hath broken down the dividing barrier of enmity. He hath brought to naught in his flesh the law of commandments framed in decrees, that in himself he might create of the two one new man, and make peace and reconcile both in one body to God through the cross, staying by means thereof their enmity. And so he came and " brought glad tidings of peace " to you " that were afar off and of peace to them that were near " : [1] because through him we both have access in one Spirit to the Father. [Ephes. ii. 11–18.]

The Promises of God are Without Repentance—the People of Israel will be Converted

Behold then at once the goodness and the severity of God : his severity towards them that have fallen—but towards thee the goodness of God, if thou abide in goodness, for else thou too shalt be cut off. And they too, if they do not abide in unbelief, will be grafted in ; for God is able to graft them in once more. Indeed, if thou hast been cut off from that which is by nature a wild olive tree, and hast been grafted contrary to nature, into the good olive tree, how much more shall these, the natural branches, be grafted back into their own olive tree ! [Rom. xi. 22–24.]

A veil has now fallen over the hearts of the Jews, but it is not forever ; the day will come when it will be taken away. For God's promises are without repentance. Throughout all the vicissitudes of its exile and of worldly history, Israel remains

---

[1] Isa. lvii. 19 ; lii. 7.

ever the people of God—stricken, but ever beloved because of its fathers.[1]

"Moses . . . was wont to place a veil over his face that the children of Israel might not gaze upon the end of that which was but passing away [2]—but their minds were hardened ; for until this present day at the reading of the Old Testament the selfsame veil remaineth, unlifted, for it is in Christ that it is done away. Nay, to this very day, when Moses is read, the veil doth lie upon their heart ; yet when their heart shall turn to the Lord, the veil is to be stripped off." [2 Cor. iii. 13–16.]

For I would not have you ignorant, brethren, of this mystery (lest ye be wise in your own conceits), that hardening in part has happened in Israel, until the fulness of the gentiles be entered in ; and thus all Israel shall be saved, according as it is written,

> There shall come from Sion the deliverer,
>   he shall banish impiety from Jacob.
> And when I take away their sins
>   this shall be to them my covenant.

As touching the gospel, indeed they are enemies for your sake, but as touching the election they are beloved for the sake of the fathers. For the gifts and the call of God are without repentance. Just as yourselves at one time disobeyed God, but now have found mercy through their disobedience, so they too have now disobeyed through the mercy shown to you, in order that they too, as it is, may find mercy. For God hath imprisoned all alike in disobedience, in order that he may have mercy on all.

O the depths of the riches and of the wisdom and of the knowledge of God ! How inscrutable are his judgments, and how untraceable his ways !

---

[1] In his first Epistle to the Thessalonians, Saint Paul tells them they have suffered of their fellow-citizens what the churches of Judaea have had to suffer on the part of the Jews—" those Jews who killed the Lord Jesus and the prophets, and drove us out, and are hateful to God and foes to all men, because they hinder our speaking salvation to the gentiles, thus filling up at all times the measure of their sins. But God's wrath hath come upon them to the uttermost " [I Thess. ii. 15–16]. It is against those of the Jews who, proud and evil as the killers of the prophets and the murderers of the Christ, were persecuting the Christians, and by their slanders made difficult the spread of the Gospel that Paul was thus indignant. He is not thinking—that is perfectly clear—of the Jewish people as such, on which subject he expresses himself altogether otherwise when he treats it formally in the Epistle to the Romans. From the very fact that " the gifts and the call of God are without repentance," this people continues " ever beloved because of its fathers." Cf. Lagrange, Epitre aux Romains, p. 266.

[2] In order that the children of Israel might not see the effulgence pass from his face. A symbol of the transitory nature of the Old Covenant.

Who hath known the mind of the Lord, or who
hath become his counsellor ?
Or who hath first given to him, that
he should be repaid ? [1]

For from him and through him and unto him are all things ; to him
be the glory forever. Amen. [Rom. xi. 25-36.]

Saint Thomas writes in his commentary on Saint John's
Gospel, in connection with the running of the two Apostles
Peter and John to the tomb of the Lord : " The two peoples,
the Jewish people and the people of the gentiles, are symbolized
at the tomb of Christ by the two Apostles. They simultaneously
run to Christ through the ages : the gentiles by their natural
law, the Jews by their written Law. The gentiles, like Peter,
who arrives second at the Sepulchre, later arrive at the knowledge of Jesus Christ ; but, like Peter, they are the first to enter.
The Jewish people, the first to know the mystery of the Redemption, will only be the last converted to the faith of Christ.
. . . Then, says the Gospel, *John went in ;* Israel shall not
remain eternally at the threshold of the Sepulchre. After
Peter shall have gone in, John himself will go in, for at the end
the Jews, they also, will be gathered into the faith." [2]

[1] Isa. xl. 13 ; Job xli. 2.   [2] *In Joan.* xviii. lect. 1.

Chapter V

BUT THE GREATEST IS CHARITY

Love is the Fulness of the Law

SUCH IS THE CONCLUSION OF ALL PAUL'S DISCUSSION OF THE
Law. It ends with the commandment of charity, in
which, as the gospel says [Matt. xxii. 40], consists all
the Law and the prophets. The aim of admonition is charity
[1 Tim. i. 5]. Love is the fulness of the Law. It is love which
enables us to accomplish truly and in fact all the other commandments. Where love is, slavery is no more. *Ubi caritas et amor,
ibi Deus est.* The love of charity—the love of God efficaciously
loved above all, and the love of one's neighbour, that is of all
men, loved in God and for God, and whom in loving we
make become to us as though they were ourselves (and these
two loves are but one single love)—the love of charity of itself
works for good. "Love and do what you want," Saint Augustine was to say. And according to the Vulgate, the verse in
the Epistle to the Romans which to-day is translated, "Charity
worketh no evil to the neighbour," should read, "charity for
the neighbour does not work evil."

Owe no man anything, save mutual charity ; for he that loveth
his neighbour hath fulfilled the Law. For,
> Thou shalt not commit adultery :
> Thou shalt not kill :
> Thou shalt not steal :
> Thou shalt not covet,
These and all other commandments are summed up in this sentence,
> Thou shalt love thy neighbour as thyself.
Charity worketh not evil to a neighbour. Charity therefore is the fulness
of the Law. [Rom. xiii. 8–10.]

Charity is God's Gift of Gifts

Charity does not exist here below without faith and hope.
But of the three theological virtues, which are given us by

grace together with gratuitous justification, it is charity which is the greatest and which deserves life eternal.

More than this, I show you a way that surpasseth all. If I speak with the tongues of men and of angels, but have no charity, I am become as sounding brass or clanging cymbal. And if I have the gift of prophecy, and comprehend all mysteries and all knowledge ; and if I have all faith so as to displace mountains, but have not charity, I am nothing. And if I bestow in doles all my goods, and if I deliver my body to the flames, but have not charity, it profiteth me nothing.

Charity is patient, is kind ; charity envieth not, is not pretentious, is not puffed up, behaveth not amiss, seeketh not her own, is not provoked, regardeth not evil ; rejoiceth not over wickedness, but rejoiceth with the truth ; beareth all things, believeth all things, hopeth all things, endureth all things.

Charity faileth never : whereas prophecyings, they shall have an end ; tongues, they shall cease ; knowledge, it shall have an end. For we know in part, and we prophesy in part ; but when the perfect is come, what is in part shall have an end. When I was a child, I spoke as a child, I felt as a child, I thought as a child ; now that I am become a man, I have made an end of childish ways. For now we see in a mirror, obscurely ; but then face to face. Now I know in part ; then shall I know fully, even as I have been fully known. So there abide faith, hope, charity, these three ; but the greatest of these is charity. [1 Cor. xiii. 1–13.]

The gift of tongues, of which Paul here speaks, was, together with the gift of prophecy, very widespread in the primitive Church. Such "powers" (*charismata*) given for the use of one's neighbour, should be strictly distinguished from sanctifying grace and from the theological virtues. And even with regard to the virtue of faith and the virtue of hope, charity is more excellent, because it will continue in heaven, whereas faith, which knows God obscurely, in the mirror of created likenesses which He uses to "declare" Himself [John i. 18] to us in our own language, will give place to the Vision, and hope will give place to Possession.

Brotherly Love

Let charity be without hypocrisy. Detest evil, cleave to good. Love one another with the affection of brothers, in honour forestalling

one another, flagging not in zeal, fervent in spirit, serving the Lord,
rejoicing in hope, patient in affliction, persevering in prayer, sharing with
the saints in their needs, practising hospitality. Bless them that persecute
you, bless and curse not. Rejoice with them that rejoice ; weep with
them that weep. Be of one mind with each other ; be not high
minded, but give yourselves over to humility. " Be not wise in your
own conceits." [1] To no man return evil for evil. " Take thought for
what is good in the sight of all men." [2] If it be possible, so far as in you
lieth, be at peace with all men. Avenge not yourselves, beloved, but
give room to the wrath of God ; for it is written, " Vengeance is mine,
I will repay, saith the Lord." [3] But " if thine enemy hunger, feed him ;
if he thirst, give him to drink ; for in so doing thou shalt heap coals of
fire upon his head." [4] Be not overcome by evil, but overcome evil
by good. [Rom. xii. 9-21.]

Feeling for justice is unconquerable in us ; charity tran-
scends it ; it does not destroy it. To forgive in full and complete measure, we must know that God makes it His affair
to redress the balance of things, and that the coals of fire which
are heaped upon the head of the unjust man make ready the
day when the evil works accumulated by him will be upset,
and when the grace of conversion will assault his heart.

Each should " bear his own burden," that is to say, have
care for the task set him by God, without making judgments
of others. And we should " bear one another's burdens,"
that is to say, forgive offences and mutually help each other
along the way.

Brethren, even if a man be taken in some offence, do ye who are
spiritual set such a one right in a spirit of gentleness, looking to thyself,
lest thou in thy turn be tempted. Bear ye one another's burdens, and
so shall ye fulfil the law of Christ. For if a man think he is somebody,
whereas he is nobody, he deludeth himself. Let each prove his own
work, and then he shall have matter for boasting in himself alone, and
not in a comparison with his neighbour. For each one shall bear his
own burdens. [Gal. vi. 1-5.]

Let none seek his own profit, but his neighbour's. [1 Cor. x. 24.]

There remaineth this : he that soweth sparingly, shall also reap
sparingly ; and he that soweth bountifully, shall also reap bountifully.

---

[1] Prov. iii. 7.   [2] Prov. iii. 4 (lxx.).
[3] Deut. xxxii. 35.   [4] Prov. xxv. 21-22.

Let each one give according as he hath determined in his own mind, not grudgingly nor from constraint, for " God loveth a cheerful giver." [1] And God is able to make all grace to abound unto you, so that having in all things all sufficiency ye may abound in every good work, as it is written

> He scattered abroad, he gave to the poor,
> his justness abideth for ever.[2]   [2 Cor. ix. 6–9.]

Faith

" Faith is the assurance of things hoped for, a conviction of things not seen. Because of it the men of old had divine testimony borne to them " [Heb. xi. 1]. The Greek words ὑπόστασις and ἔλεγχος can be otherwise translated, and the rendering of the Vulgate, followed by Saint Thomas Aquinas, seems to me preferable : " Faith is the substance of things hoped for, a certification of things not seen."

This definition means that faith is the hidden reality of the things we hope for, certified to us by God's testimony, without our seeing those things.

In the famous chapter of the Epistle to the Hebrews from whence is drawn this formula, Saint Paul heaps praise upon the faith of the just men of old, who awaited the Saviour, but have not known Him. They had implicit faith in that which has later been more fully revealed. Saint Paul in this connection points out the primary truths which contain in themselves all else, and on which this faith rested.

Without faith, it is impossible to please God ; for he that approacheth unto God must believe that he doth exist, and is a rewarder to those who seek him.   [Heb. xi. 6.]

To so much, at least, must consent the inner certainty of those who cannot know in its fulness the truth as Christ revealed it for all time, in order that they may have implicit faith in all else and be in God's grace. And it is by a gift of God that such believe, for it is here a question of a saving God, which goes beyond the reason's natural power of apprehension. This minimum of faith content is necessary for salvation, whatever may be, from the psychological point of view, the

[1] Prov. xxii. 8 (lxx.).   [2] Ps. cxii. (cxi.) 9.

degree of clarity in which the soul is conscious thereof. For supernatural faith is the prerequisite of the supernatural loves of God, of the charity which efficaciously loves God above all things, like a friend who calls us to share his life.

Moreover, Paul clearly holds that faith, which of itself seeks to blossom out into love, can nevertheless, through the corruption of sin, exist in a soul without charity : for even while they believe in the truths of faith, Christians can be lost by losing charity. Of those Christians who do not take care of their own, he tells us that by their actions they give the lie to faith, and that they are worse than those without faith. "If any man provideth not for his own, and especially for his family, he hath denied the faith, and is worse than an unbeliever" [1 Tim. v. 8]. And of the Christian widow who gives herself over to the joys of the flesh, he tells us that she is dead in her soul. "She that is wanton, liveth in death" [1 Tim. v. 6]. It is to the faithful that he says, "Be not deceived, God is not mocked. For whatsoever a man soweth, that shall he reap. . . ." [Gal. vi. 7]. But indeed the faith of which he speaks, both in the text from the Epistle to the Hebrews which is here reproduced, and in all the others so far cited, is always faith joined to charity, the faith which "worketh by love" [cf. Gal. v. 6].

Such was the faith of the just men of old.

Now faith is the substance of things hoped for, a certification of things not seen ; for because of it the men of old had divine testimony borne to them.

Through faith we know that the ages were fashioned by God's word, so that from naught visible that which is visible hath come to be.

Through faith Abel offered to God a better sacrifice than Cain, in virtue whereof it was testified of him that he was just, since God gave testimony concerning his gifts ; and in virtue of the same faith he speaketh still, though dead.[1]

Through faith was Henoch taken away, so that he saw not death ; and "he was not found, for God had taken him away" : for even before he was taken away he received the testimony that "he had pleased God." [2] And without faith it is impossible to please him ;

---

[1] After the death of Abel his blood made appeal to the justice of God, and the appeal was heard.
[2] Cf. Gen. v. 22–24.

for he that approacheth unto God must believe that he does exist, and is a rewarder to those who seek him.

Through faith Noah, having been instructed concerning things not yet visible, dutifully prepared an ark for the salvation of his house ; and in virtue thereof he judged the world, and became an heir of the justness which is based on faith.

Through faith was Abraham obedient to the call to go forth to a place which he was to receive as an inheritance ; and he went forth, not knowing whither he was going. Through faith he sojourned in the land of promise as in a foreign country, dwelling in tents with Isaac and Jacob, the fellow-heirs of the same promise ; for he looked to the city with firm foundations, whereof God is the architect and builder. Through faith, too, Sara received power for the conception of seed, in spite of her age, because she looked on him who had given the promise as faithful. Hence there hath sprung from a single man— and him as good as dead—issue " like the stars of heaven for number, and like the countless sands on the sea-shore." [1]

In faith all these died without receiving the promises, but only seeing and greeting them from afar, and acknowledging that they were but " strangers and sojourners on earth." For those who say such things make it plain that they search for a fatherland. And if they were thinking of that whence they had come forth, they would have found opportunity to return ; but as it is, they long for a better one— that is, a heavenly. Whence God is not ashamed to be called their God, for he hath prepared for them a city.

Through faith " Abraham offered Isaac when he was put to the test," and he who had received the promises offered his only son—he to whom it had been said, " Through Isaac thy seed shall be reckoned." [2] For he reasoned that God hath power to raise up even from among the dead, whence he received him back for a type. Through faith Isaac blessed Jacob and Esau, in regard to things future. Through faith Jacob, when dying, blessed each of the sons of Joseph, and " bowed in worship over the top of his staff." [3] Through faith Jacob, when nearing his end, made mention of the departure of the sons of Israel, and gave orders concerning his own bones.

Through faith Moses " was kept in concealment " by his parents " for three months " after his birth, because " they saw that the child was comely " ; and they were not afraid of the king's decree. Through faith did " Moses, when he had grown to man's estate," [4] refuse to be

---

[1] Gen. xxii. 17 ; xxxii. 12.   [2] Gen. xxi. 12.
[3] Gen. xlvii. 31 (lxx.).   [4] Exod. ii. 2 ; 11.

called the son of Pharaoh's daughter, preferring to bear shame with the people of God rather than to enjoy a fleeting experience of sin. He deemed the shame of Christ to be greater wealth than the treasures of the Egyptians ; for he looked forward to the reward. Through faith he left Egypt, having no fear of the king's wrath, but holding to his purpose, as seeing him who is invisible. Through faith he carried out the Passover, and the sprinkling of blood, so that the destroyer of the first-born might not touch them. Through faith they traversed the Red Sea as through dry land, whereas the Egyptians, making trial of it, were swallowed up. Through faith fell the walls of Jericho, after they had been for seven days encompassed. Through faith the harlot Rahab was not destroyed with the disobedient, because she had received the spies in peace.

What shall I say further ? Time will fail me if I go on to tell of Gideon, Barak, Samson, Jephthah, David, Samuel, and the prophets ; who through faith subdued kingdoms, practised justness, received promises, closed the mouth of lions, extinguished the might of fire, escaped the edge of the sword, came to strength out of weakness, were strong in battle, routed armies of alien foes. Women received back their dead by a resurrection. Others were broken to death, refusing to accept release, that they might attain a better resurrection : others had trial of mockery and stripes, yea, even of fetters and imprisonment : they were stoned, they were tempted, they were sawn asunder, they died by the death of the sword, they went about in sheepskins and goatskins, in need, tribulation, and ill-treatment—of whom the world was not worthy—wandering in deserts and mountains and caves and holes of the earth. And all these, though through their faith they won approving testimony, yet did not receive the fulfilment of the promise, for God had something greater in view in regard of us, so that they could not come to perfection without us. [Heb. xi. 1-40.]

Hope

The whole of Paul's teaching is suffused and exalted by the virtue of hope. Yet he devotes thereto less explicit development than he does to the other theological virtues. This is indeed because, in his teaching as in Christian life, hope plays a rôle so profoundly " existential " that it is like some vegetative force which supplies us life, and which we feel no compelling need to make an object of explicit speculation. Yet everywhere it is present. It even enters into the Pauline definition of faith. Faith is the substance of things hoped for.

Everything we have received, we have received *in hope*—
in hope of life eternal—because we are but a rough outline
of what we shall some day be, and because all the life of the
gifts of grace in us is a movement and an impetus toward that
which we shall possess only when we shall see God face to face,
"knowing then as we are known." That is basic in Saint
Paul's thought. The just man lives by faith ; therefore he
also lives by hope. For, as we have seen in connection with
justification by faith, the confidence of faith—that is to say,
hope—is that divine assurance which replaces in us any illusion
of human security. Hope is distinguished from possession,
which is real only at the vision, so that properly speaking we
do not yet *possess* anything that we have. To anyone who
relies entirely upon faith, to one who goes forward with closed
eyes, knowing that of himself he is nothing able, there is no
other power but hope on which to build and advance—for
to-morrow, and even for the present moment—and there is
no other infallible guarantee but the help of the all-powerful
God and the merits of Jesus Christ, in Whom such a one has
placed his confidence.

Creation with eager straining awaiteth the manifestation of the
children of God. [If it] was made subject to vanity, [this was in order
to live] in the hope that creation itself shall be freed from its slavery to
corruption unto the freedom of the glory of the children of God. . . .
[And ourselves too], who have the first fruits of the Spirit, we groan
within ourselves while awaiting adoption, the redemption of our body.
[Rom. viii. 19-23.]

For in hope we are saved. And hope beheld is not hope : for how can
a man hope what he beholdeth ? But if we hope for what we behold
not, we await in patience. [Rom. viii. 24-25.]

Such is the confidence we have through Christ towards God. Not
as though we were of ourselves sufficient to think anything, as from
ourselves, but our sufficiency is from God. [2 Cor. iii. 4-5.]

One body and one Spirit, as also ye are called in one hope, that
of your calling. [Ephes. iv. 4.]

Let us temperately and justly and piously live in the present world,
looking for the blessed hope and manifestation of the glory of our great
God and Saviour, Jesus Christ. [Tit. ii. 12-13.]

For his sake I have suffered the loss of all things and count them
but dung, in order that I may gain Christ and be found in him. . . .

Not that I have already secured this, or am already made perfect. Rather I press on, in the hope that I may lay hold of that for which Christ hath laid hold of me. Brethren, I do not count myself to have laid hold of it already. Yet one thing I do; I forget what is behind, and strain forward to what is before, and press on towards the goal, to gain the reward of God's heavenly call in Christ Jesus. [Philip. iii. 8, 12–14.]

If only ye hold by the faith, well-grounded and steadfast, without swerving from the hope of the glad tidings which ye have heard. . . . The hope that is laid up for you in heaven . . . Christ within you, your hope of glory. [Colos. i. 23 ; v. 27.]

Whatsoever things were written aforetime were written for our instruction, that through patience and through the comfort of the scriptures we may have hope. [Rom. xv. 4.]

Through whom [Jesus Christ] we have obtained our access by faith into this grace wherein we stand and exult in the hope of the glory of God. And not only so, but we exult in our tribulations also, knowing that tribulation worketh endurance, and endurance experience, and experience hope. And " hope doth not prove false," for the charity of God is poured forth in our hearts through the Holy Spirit who hath been given to us, so surely as Christ, while we were yet weak, died in due season, on behalf of the impious. . . .

For if when we were enemies we were reconciled to God through the death of his Son, all the more, once reconciled, shall we be saved by his life. And not only so, but we exult in God through our Lord Jesus Christ, through whom we have even now received this reconciliation. [Rom. v. 2–6, 10–11.]

Moses was faithful *in* his whole house, as servant to testify what was to be spoken ; but Christ as Son *over* his house : which house we are, if we hold firm to the end our confidence and the boasting of our hope. [Heb. iii. 5–6.]

Since therefore, brethren, we have full freedom to enter the sanctuary in virtue of the blood of Jesus, a new and living way which he hath inaugurated for us through the veil, that is to say, his flesh, and since we have " a great High Priest over the house of God,"[1] let us come forward with a true heart in full assurance of faith, purified through the besprinkling of our heart from an evil conscience, and with body cleansed in pure water. Let us hold fast inflexibly to the confession of hope, for faithful is he who hath given the promise. [Heb. x. 19–23.]

God is not unjust so as to forget your works and the love which ye have shown towards his name, when ye ministered, and still minister,

---

[1] Zech. vi. 11 ff. ; Num. xii. 7.

to the saints. But we desire that each one of you should show the same zeal for the fulness of hope unto the end, that ye may not grow dull, but rather be imitators of those who by faith and perseverance inherit the promises.

For when God gave Abraham promise, since he could swear by none greater, he sware by himself, saying :

I will surely bless thee, and I will surely multiply thee.

And so, after patient waiting, he attained the promise. For men swear by one greater than themselves, and the oath giveth them a surety beyond all contradiction. Hence God, wishing to put before the heirs of the promise still more clearly his unchangeable will, gave warrant with an oath. So that by two unchangeable things [the promise and the oath], wherein God cannot speak falsely, we have a sure consolation, who have sought refuge in seizing the hope offered to us. In it we have a safe and secure anchor of the soul, " one which reacheth even behind the veil," [1] whither, as Forerunner, Jesus hath entered on our behalf, having become " a High Priest for ever after the manner of Melchisedech." [2] [Heb. vi. 10–20.]

Let us, therefore, approach with confidence to the throne of grace, so that we may receive mercy, and find grace to help us in due season. [Heb. iv. 16.]

---

[1] Cf. Levit. xvi. 2 ; 12.   [2] Cf. Ps. cx. (cix.) 4.

CHAPTER VI

CHRIST THE REDEEMER

The Divinity of Christ

THE EXPRESSION PAUL USES IN THE EPISTLE TO THE HEBREWS when he says that Christ is the very " impress " of the " substance " or of the essence of God has its equivalent and its explanation in the Epistle to the Colossians, wherein Christ is called " the image of the unseen God, first-born before every creature " [Colos. i. 15], and where it is said that " in him dwelleth all the fulness of the Godhead corporeally " [Colos. ii. 9]. He is the impress of the divine substance or essence which he has in common with His Father. He is the first-born, because He is the Son externally conceived, in Whom and by Whom all things have been made [Colos. i. 16–17] ; and He is also, as a man, and by His resurrection " the first-born from the dead " [Colos. i. 18].

In him dwelleth all the fulness of the Godhead corporeally : and in him ye attain your fulness, who is the head of every principality and power. In him again it is that ye were circumcised with a circumcision not wrought with hands, the stripping off of your fleshly body, in the circumcision which is of Christ.

Along with him ye were buried in baptism : along with him also ye had your resurrection through your faith in the power of God, who raised him up from the dead. Even thus when ye were dead in your transgressions and in the uncircumcision of your flesh, did he bring you to life along with Christ, freely pardoning us all our transgressions and washing out the handwriting that was against us, with its decrees. Yea, Christ lifted it clean away, nailing it to the cross ; thus he cast off the principalities and powers, and made open show of them, leading them away in triumph by force of it. [Colos. ii. 9–15.]

It is by virtue of the very order of nature, over which invisibly preside the angelic spirits (the " principalities " and the " powers "), and by virtue of the natural laws in accordance with which our acts bear their fruit, that the accomplishment of the desires of the flesh (the uncircumcision of your flesh) brings death to souls. In restoring life to us and purifying us according to a spiritual circumcision, Christ, Who by reason of this divine nature is the chief of all the angelic spirits, triumphed over them through the Cross, and made open show of them, because He triumphed over that very order of natural concatenations which linked us to death because of our faults, that order of which created spirits are the guardians, and to which false sages asked the Colossians to link themselves anew by superstitious observances, in place of rejoicing at having been freed of the sentence inscribed in it against them—freed by the Cross and by the blood of the Just.

He is the image of the unseen God, first-born before every creature. For in him were created all things in heaven and on earth, things seen and things unseen, whether thrones or dominations or principalities or powers—all creation is through him and unto him. And himself is prior to all, and in him all things hold together. He again is the head of the body, the Church : it is he who is the beginning, the first-born from the dead, that so among all he himself may stand first. For in him it hath pleased the Father that all the fulness should dwell, and through him to reconcile all things to himself, alike the things on earth and the things in heaven, making peace through the blood of his cross. [Colos. i. 15–20.]

[He is] our great God and Saviour Christ Jesus, [Whose] glory's manifestation we look for. [Tit. ii. 13.]

He, though he was by nature God, yet did not set great store on his equality with God : rather, he emptied himself by taking the nature of a slave and becoming like unto men. And after he had appeared in outward form as man, he humbled himself by obedience unto death, yea, unto death upon a cross. Wherefore God hath exalted him above the highest, and hath bestowed on him the name which is above every name ; that at the name of Jesus " every knee should bend " in heaven, on earth, and under the earth, and that " every tongue should confess " that " Jesus Christ is Lord," [1] to the glory of God the Father. [Phil. ii. 6–11.]

[Christ is] over all, God blessed for ever. [Rom. ix. 5.]

For him and through him and unto him are all things. [Rom. xi. 36.]

---

[1] Cf. Isa. xlv. 23.

Christ's Work

Christ is true God, but He is also true Man. And it is through the work which such a Man has wrought, in dying for those He loves, and who are all men, and in giving for them His blood that He has been made Mediator and Redeemer.

There is " one mediator between God and men, himself man, Christ Jesus, who gave himself a ransom for all men." [1 Tim. ii. 6.]

Our Lord Jesus Christ gave himself for our sins that he might save us from the wickedness of the present world. [Gal. i. 4.]

In him we have redemption through his blood, the forgiveness of our transgressions, according to the riches of his grace. [Ephes. i. 7.]

Him that knew not sin, for our sakes he made sin, that in him we might become the justness of God. [2 Cor. v. 21 ; cf. Gal. iii. 13–14 ; see p. 63.]

As through Adam sin and death came to the whole of mankind, so through Jesus Christ justice and grace come to all mankind. Paul here decisively affirms the natural unity of the human species, a necessary presupposition for Christianity and the basis of the unity of redemption.

Therefore as through one man sin came into the world, and through sin death, and thus death spread to all men, because all had sinned— for until the Law sin was in the world, and sin is not imputed where there is no law ; yet death reigned from Adam till Moses even over such as had not sinned after the likeness of the transgression of Adam,[1] who is a figure of him that was to be.

But not as the offence was the act of grace. For if by reason of the offence of the one the many died, much more have the grace of God and the gift given in the grace of the one man Jesus Christ been lavished upon the many. Nor again was it with the gift as with the sin [both coming] from one man. The sentence ensuing upon the one man's sin was unto condemnation, but the act of grace which ensueth upon many offences is unto justification. For if by reason of the offence of the one man death hath reigned through the one man, much more shall

---

[1] " After the likeness of the transgression of Adam," *i.e.* not only against the natural law, but against a positive commandment of God, head of the supernatural order (into which Adam had been constituted from his creation).

they who receive the abundance of the grace and of the gift of justness reign in life through the one Jesus Christ.

So, then, as through one offence condemnation came to all men, so also through a single justifying act there cometh to all men life-giving justification. As through the disobedience of the one man the many were constituted sinners, so also through the obedience of the one the many shall be constituted just. The Law was interposed that offence might be multiplied. But where sin hath been multiplied, grace hath abounded yet more, that, as sin hath reigned in death, so also grace may reign through justness unto life everlasting through Jesus Christ our Lord. [Rom. v. 12–20.]

The Mediator of the New Covenant

The Angels and Moses were the mediators of the Old Testament. Christ, mediator of the New Testament, is the Son of God, the heir of all things. He is superior to the Angels.

God, having spoken of old to the fathers through the prophets by many partial revelations and in various ways, in these last days hath spoken to us by one who is Son, whom he hath set up as heir of all things ; by whom also he created the ages. He, being the effulgence of his glory, and the very impress (seal) of his substance, sustaineth all things by God's word of power ; and having made a cleansing from sin, " hath taken his seat at the right hand " [1] of Majesty on high, having become much greater than the angels, as the name which he hath inherited surpasseth theirs.

For to which of the angels hath he ever said :
    Thou art my son ; this day I have begotten thee ? [2]
Or again :
    I will be to him Father, and he will be to me Son ? [3]
And again, when he bringeth the Firstborn into the world, he saith :
    Let the angels of God worship him.[4]   [Heb. i. 1–6.]

As a man, he has been made but little lower than the Angels. The phrase in the psalm, " Thou hast put all things beneath his feet," does not apply to man—that is only too clear—unless to man in Him who is the perfect Man, and Who has passed through suffering for the salvation of His brothers.

---

[1] Cf. Ps. cx. (cix.) 1. [2] Ps. ii. 7.
[3] II Sam. (Kings) vii. 14. [4] Ps. xcvii. (xcvi.) 7.

7

Not to the angels hath he made subject the future world of which we speak. Rather hath one somewhere testified as follows :

> What is man that thou art mindful of him ?
> or the son of man that thou visitest him ?
> Thou hast made him but a little lower than the angels,
> with glory and honour thou hast crowned him :
> And thou hast set him over the works of thy hands :
> thou hast put all things beneath his feet.[1]

Now in subjecting all things to him he left nothing that is not subject to him. And yet, at present, we do not see all things made subject ! But him who was made a little lower than the angels, even Jesus, we see crowned with glory and honour because of the sufferings of death, that he, by God's grace, might taste death on behalf of all.

For it behoved him on account of whom all things are, and through whom all things are, when he was bringing many sons to glory, to make perfect through suffering the author of their salvation. [Heb. ii. 5–10.]

For we are partakers in Christ, provided only that we hold firm our first confidence even to the end. [Heb. iii. 14.]

He is superior to Moses.

Wherefore, holy brethren, sharers in a heavenly call, give heed to the Apostle and High Priest of our confession, Jesus—who is " true " to him that hath made him, even as was " Moses in all his house." [2] But, as compared with Moses, Jesus is to be esteemed worthy of greater honour, even as the builder hath greater honour than the house he hath built. For every house is built by some one, but the builder of the universe is God. And Moses was faithful *in* his whole house, as servant to testify what was to be spoken ; but Christ as Son *over* his house : which house we are, if we hold firm to the end our confidence and the boasting of our hope. [Heb. iii. 1–6.]

Christ is the priest of priests. His eternal priesthood is superior to the priesthood of Aaron.

Since, then, we have a great High Priest who hath passed through the heavens, Jesus the Son of God, let us hold firmly to what we confess. For we have not a high priest who is unable to realize in himself our weaknesses, but rather one who hath been tried in every way like ourselves, short of sin. [Heb. iv. 14–16.]

---

[1] Ps. viii.　　　[2] Num. xii. 7.

For every high priest taken from among men is appointed as a representative of men in the things that refer to God, that he may offer gifts and sacrifices for sins ; as one who can be mild with the ignorant and erring since he himself is encompassed with weakness, and because of it must make offerings for sin, not merely on behalf of the people, but also for himself. And none taketh to himself the honour but one who hath been called by God, as was Aaron.

So, too, Christ did not appoint himself to the honour of becoming High Priest, but he who said to him :

Thou art my Son ; this day I have begotten thee.[1] As he elsewhere saith :

Thou art Priest for ever after the manner of Melchisedech.[2]

In the days of his flesh he offered up prayers and supplications to him who could save him from death, with a loud cry and tears, and was heard because of his devout submission : and though he was Son, he learned obedience from that which he suffered : himself made perfect, he became for all who obey him the author of eternal salvation, designated by God as High Priest " after the manner of Melchisedech." Heb. v. 1-10.]

For this " Melchisedech, king of Salem, Priest of God Most High, who met Abraham when he was returning from the defeat of the kings and blessed him, to whom also Abraham gave tithes of all things," who is, in the first place, set forth as " king of justice," and in the next place, as " king of Salem," that is, " king of peace," who is fatherless, motherless, without genealogy, without beginning of days or end of life, but made like unto the Son of God—he remaineth " Priest for ever." . . .[3]

Now if perfection had been reached through the levitical priesthood —for the people hath received a law based upon it—what would be the need that another " priest after the manner of Melchisedech " should be set up, and that there should be question of one not after the manner of Aaron ? When the priesthood is changed, there taketh place also of necessity a change of the law. For he in view of whom all this is said belongeth to another tribe, from which no one doth service at the altar ; it is, in fact, well known that our Lord is sprung from Juda—a tribe about which Moses said nothing that would refer to priests.

And the matter is still more abundantly clear if another Priest is set up after the very likeness of Melchisedech, who is not become so

---

[1] Ps. ii. [2] Ps. cx. (cix.) 4.

[3] Cf. Gen. xiv. 17-20, and Ps. cx. (cix.) 4.

in virtue of the law of a fleshly commandment, but in virtue of th
power of an indissoluble life. For it is testified of him :

Thou art a Priest for ever after the manner of Melchisedech. O
the one hand there is here a rejection of an earlier command becaus
of its powerlessness and uselessness—for indeed the law brough
nothing to perfection—and on the other hand it is the introductio
of a better hope, through which we draw nigh unto God. . . .

And they have been made priests many in number, because prevente
by death from remaining : but he, because he remaineth for eve
hath an unchangeable priesthood. Wherefore he can at all tim
save those who approach God through him, since he liveth alway
to make intercession for them.

Such was the High Priest fitted for our needs—holy, guileles
undefiled, set apart from sinners and made higher than the heaven
who hath not need daily, like the high priests, to offer sacrifice fir
of all for his own sins, and then for those of the people : for this latte
he did once for all when he offered himself. [Heb. vii. 1–3, 11–1￢
23–27.]

In the degree that the mediation of Christ and His priesthoo
are superior to the mediation of Moses and the priesthood o
Aaron, in that degree is the new Covenant superior to the ol

He hath attained to a ministry so much the more excellent, as th
testament is better whereof he is Mediator, which hath been enacte
on the basis of more important promises. For if that first had bee
without defect, place for a second would not be sought. For he ￢
censuring them when he saith :

Behold the days are coming, saith the Lord
　　when I shall make with the house of Israel
And with the house of Juda,
　　a new covenant, not according to the covenant
Which I made with their fathers on the day when
　　　I took their hand,
　　to lead them forth from the land of Egypt.
For they did not abide by my covenant,
　　and I had no regard for them, saith the Lord.
For this is the covenant which I will set up with
　　the house of Israel
　　after those days, saith the Lord :
I will put my laws into their mind,
　　and upon their hearts will I write them :

And I will be to them a God,
    and they shall be to me a people.
And they shall not teach every man his fellow-citizen,
    and every man his brother, saying, Know the Lord :
Because all shall know me,
    from the least to the greatest among them.
For I will be compassionate towards their evildoings,
    and their sins I will remember no more.[1]

When he saith a " new " covenant, he hath made obsolete the former covenant ; that which is obsolete and old is nigh unto disappearance. [Heb. viii. 6-13.]

Christ, having appeared as High Priest of the good things to come, hath entered into the sanctuary once for all through the greater and more perfect tabernacle, not made by hands, that is, not belonging to this creation, nor again in virtue of the blood of goats and calves, but of his own blood, having thus secured everlasting redemption. For if the blood of goats and bulls and the sprinkled ashes of a heifer sanctify the unclean unto purity of flesh, how much more will the blood of Christ, who through his eternal Spirit hath offered himself un-blemished unto God, purify our conscience from dead works unto the service of the living God ?

For this, then, is he the Mediator of a new testament, that whereas a death hath taken place unto the redemption of the transgression under the first testament, those who are called may receive eternal inheritance according to the promise. For where there is a testament, the death of the testator must be established, for a testament is valid only in regard to the dead, but hath no force as long as the testator liveth.

Hence even the first testament was not inaugurated without blood ; for when every command had been read forth for all the people by Moses according to the Law, he took the blood of the calves and the goats together with water and scarlet wool and hyssop, and sprinkled the book itself and all the people, saying, " This is the blood of the covenant which God hath commanded you." [2] The tabernacle, too, and all the vessels for divine worship he sprinkled likewise with blood, and with blood is almost everything purified according to the Law, and without the shedding of blood there is no pardon.

It was necessary, therefore, that the copies of the heavenly realities should be purified by such things as these ; but the heavenly realities

---

[1] Jerem. xxxi. (xxxviii.) 31-34.   [2] Exod. xxiv. 8.

themselves require better sacrifices than these. For Christ hath not entered into a sanctuary made by hands, a mere type of the true, but into heaven itself, to appear now before the face of God on our behalf ; nor yet to offer himself often, even as the High Priest entereth annually into the sanctuary with blood not his own, for then he must needs have often suffered since the beginning of the world. But now once for all at the close of the ages hath he appeared unto the abolition of sin by his sacrifice. And as it is appointed to all men once to die, and thereafter cometh judgment, so also with Christ, offered once "to bear the sins of many," [1] appear a second time with no part in sin unto salvation for those who wait for him. [Heb. ix. 11-28.]

For it is impossible that the blood of bulls and goats should take away sin. Hence he saith, when entering into the world :

> Sacrifice and offering thou hast not desired,
>> but a body thou hast prepared for me.
> In holocausts and sin-offerings thou hast taken no pleasure :
>> then I said : Behold, I am come
> (in the volume so it is written of me)
>> to do, O God, thy will.[2] [Heb. x. 4-7.]

By a single offering he hath for ever perfected those who are made holy. [Heb. x. 14.]

Let us go forth to Him outside the Camp

It is not what we eat, which the Jews separated into pure and impure, it is grace that makes a pure heart.

Jesus Christ is the same yesterday and to-day, yea, and for ever. Do not be led away by manifold and strange teachings, for it is good that the heart be made firm by grace and not by foods, from which they had no profit who occupied themselves therein. [Heb. xiii. 8-9.]

The Jewish altar was inside the Tabernacle of the Temple of Jerusalem—inclosed within a people and bound to its national destiny. The Christian altar is without, because the death of Christ, being the perfect sacrifice and the perfect reparation, has abrogated the ancient sacrifices and carried salvation to the whole world. He suffered without the city. Let us leave behind the Judaic worship and the ceremonial observances of the Old Testament, which were figures of reality.

[1] Isa. liii. 12.   [2] Ps. xl. (xxxix.) 6-8.

And let us follow Jesus without the city, to suffer with Him, in the hope of the abiding city to come.

We have an altar from which they are entitled to eat who serve the Tabernacle. For the bodies of the animals " are burned outside the camp, whose blood is carried by the High Priest into the sanctuary as an offering for sin." [1] Therefore Jesus also, that he might purify the people by his own blood, suffered outside the gate. Let us then go forth to him " outside the camp," bearing his shame ; for we have here no abiding city, but seek for that which is to come. [Heb. xiii. 10–14.]

Now may the God of peace, who hath brought up from among the dead the great " pastor of the sheep, in virtue of the blood of the eternal covenant," [2] even our Lord Jesus, may he equip you perfectly with every good thing unto carrying out his will, while he himself accomplisheth in you what is pleasing to him, through Jesus Christ, to whom be glory for ever and ever. Amen. [Heb. xiii. 20–21.]

---

[1] Levit. xvi. 27.   [2] Isa. lxiii. 11 ; Zech. ix. 11.

Chapter VII

THE ECONOMY OF SALVATION

The Eucharist

The cup of blessing which we bless, is it not fellowship in the blood of Christ? The bread which we break, is it not fellowship in the body of Christ? We many are one bread, one body, for we all partake of the one bread.—1 Cor. x. 16–17.

I N SAINT PAUL'S DAY THE CELEBRATION OF THE EUCHARIST ordinarily took place after the evening meal, as at the Lord's supper. The faithful had from time to time formed the habit of carrying their suppers to the home of that one of them at whose house took place the celebration, and this brought with it some disorder. In the first chapter of the Epistle to the Corinthians, Paul exhorts the faithful to desist from this practice, and each one to take his meal at home, before gathering together for the Eucharist.

It is at the outset of the passage quoted below that appears the famous phrase, " Oportet haereses esse—there must be factions." It is here a question of the parties which had formed among the faithful at Corinth and which continued to divide the faithful even when they assembled for the Agape or for the Eucharist. Later on the word was understood as applying to divisions with regard to the faith itself, to heresies, properly so-called, something which Paul had not here in view. Yet the extension of meaning does keep within the direction of Pauline thought.

Now, while laying the above charge upon you, I do not commend your meeting together, not for the better but rather for the worse. In the first place I hear that when ye come together to church there are divisions among you, and in part I believe it. For there must even be factions among you, that those of tried virtue may become manifest among you. When ye meet together, then, it is not possible to eat the Lord's supper ; for at the repast each one taketh first his own supper, and one is hungry and another drinketh overmuch. Have ye not homes in which to eat and drink ? Or do ye despise the church of God, and put to shame the needy ? What am I to say to you ? Am I to praise you ? In this I praise you not.

For I have received from the Lord, as I have also delivered to you, that the Lord Jesus, on the night wherein he was being betrayed, took bread, and giving thanks brake and said, " This is my body on your behalf ; this do ye in remembrance of me." In like manner after the supper he took the cup saying, " This cup is the new covenant in my blood ; this do ye, as often as ye drink thereof, in remembrance of me." For as often as ye eat this bread and drink of the cup, ye proclaim the death of the Lord, until he come. So that whoever eateth the bread or drinketh of the cup of the Lord unworthily, shall be guilty of the body and of the blood of the Lord. But let a man prove himself, and so let him eat of the bread, and drink of the cup ; for he that eateth and drinketh without distinguishing the body from other food, eateth and drinketh judgment to himself. Therefore many among you are weak and sickly, and not a few are fallen asleep. Did we examine ourselves we should not thus be judged ; still, in what we are thus judged by the Lord, we are being chastised to save us from condemnation with the world. [1 Cor. xi. 17–32.]

There are many sicknesses and deaths in the world which temporally punish men for not distinguishing from earthly food the Body and Blood of the Saviour, nor from profane realities His mystical body.

The Mystical Body

As in our one body we have many members, and all the members have not the same function, even so we many are one body in Christ, and members each of the other. But we have gifts which vary according to the grace that hath been given us, whether of prophecy, to be used according to the proportions of our faith ; or of ministry, in ministering ; or again he that teaches, in teaching ; he that exhorteth, in exhortations ; he that dispenseth, in single-heartedness; he that presideth, in zeal ; he that showeth mercy, in cheerfulness. [Rom. xii. 4–8.]

And " he hath subjected all things beneath his feet," [1] and given

---

[1] Ps. viii. 6.

him for supreme head to the church, which is his body, the fulness
of him who is wholly fulfilled in all. [Ephes. i. 22-23.]

This one and indivisible body which the faithful form in
Christ is the body of Christ Himself, the extension of the
Incarnate Word, " Jesus Christ, spilled over and conveyed "
(Bossuet). Hence the Church is a visible body but a body
whose constitutive reality is essentially mysterious, since it is
the body—made up of the multitude of those who believe—
of Christ invisibly present in them in order to communicate
to them His life of grace. From this arises the traditional
expression, *mystical body of Christ*. Paul teaches this doctrine
of the mystical body in connection with the diversity of
functions in the Church, and in order to insist on the organic
unity of that body which Christ's sacrifice consecrates to God
and which is fed by the food of the Eucharist, as well as to insist
on the fraternal charity and holiness toward which should
tend all the members of such a body. And at the same time
he makes us to some extent feel the depths of the mystery of
the Church, which is but one with the mystery of the
Redemption.

The visible unity of the mystical body, made manifest in
Baptism, in the profession of faith, and in discipline, is the visible
and human instrument in the world of a life divine and hidden
which is not of the world—for it is the life of grace, the life
given by the blood of Christ—and in the invisible unity thereof
the Spirit of God prepares sons for God.

The various functions all of which Paul joins to the organic
unity of the mystical body are at once the functions of the
ordinary ministry and those of extraordinary gifts, so widespread—notably the gift of tongues [cf. 1 Cor. xiv. 1-33]—in
the primitive Church. These special gifts or powers (*charismata*)
are given, not, like the virtues of faith, hope and charity and
the other gifts that proceed from sanctifying grace, to make
him who receives them a participant in eternal life, but to help
here and now in the instruction and the encouragement of
others. Paul here emphasizes them more because human weakness was tempted to misdirect them toward a disproportioned
individualism, and because they require a discernment between

that which truly comes from the Spirit of God and that which comes from a purely human exaltation. "Now there are varieties of gifts, but the same Spirit. . . . But to each is given the manifestation of the Spirit for the general profit." [1 Cor. xii. 4 ; 7.]

For as the body is one and hath many members, and all the members of the body, many as they are, form one body, so also it is with Christ. For in one Spirit all we, whether Jews or Greeks, whether slaves or free, were baptized into one body ; and were all given to drink of one Spirit. Now the body is not one member, but many. If the foot say, Because I am not a hand, I am not of the body ; not for all that doth it cease to be of the body. And if the ear say, Because I am not an eye, I am not of the body ; not for all that doth it cease to be the body. If the body were all eye, where would be the sense of hearing ? If it were all hearing, where would be the sense of smell ? As it is, God hath set each several member in the body according as he willed. And if they were all a single member, where would be the body ? But, as it is, there are many members, yet one body. And the eye cannot say to the hand, I have no need of thee ; or again the head to the feet, I have no need of you.

Nay, much rather, those members of the body which seem to be weaker are still necessary, and those which we deem the less honourable in the body we surround with especial honour, and our uncomely parts receive especial comeliness, whereas our comely parts have no need thereof. Yea, God hath so compounded the body as to give especial honour where it was lacking, that there may be no schism in the body, but that the members may have a common care for each other. And if one member suffereth, all the members suffer therewith ; if a member be honoured, all the members rejoice therewith.

Now ye are the body of Christ, and severally his members. And God hath appointed sundry in the Church, first apostles, secondly prophets, thirdly teachers ; then there are miracles, then gifts of healing, aptitude to succour or to govern, and divers kinds of tongues. Are all apostles ? Are all prophets ? Are all teachers ? Are all workers of miracles ? Have all gifts of healing ? Do all speak with "tongues " ? Do all interpret ? Nay, covet ye the gifts that are greater. [1 Cor. xii. 11-31.]

The highest of the charismata is the gift of prophecy [1 Cor. xiv. 1-33] (Paul remarks concerning it that the prophets remain masters of themselves—" prophetic gifts are under the control of prophets "—in contrast to the frenzy which possesses pseudo-prophets).

But in comparison to charity, prophecy itself is nothing.[1] Charismata can exist in sinners ; charity is the very life in us of the most holy God. The mystical body is made up of just men and of sinners, but one baptized who has lost grace no longer really lives by the soul of the mystical body ; he is a dead member, a "dead man who lives." Whereas one unbaptized, if he is justified by implicit faith in Christ—as were in other times those just men to whom the Epistle to the Hebrews pays tribute, or those Gentiles who, because they will have fulfilled the commandments of the Law by following an upright conscience, will judge the circumcised who transgress the Law [Rom. ii. 14 ; ii. 27]—receives in him, by means of a hidden participation, a certain inflowing of the soul of the mystical body, and hence it happens that he belongs invisibly to this visible body. The soul of the mystical body consists essentially in sanctifying grace (which, when it is the grace of the sacraments, has eminent efficacy and properties specific for incorporation in and configuration with Christ) ; and it is toward the growth and increase of faith and charity, up to that complete development of Christ's body wherein all His members will know fully the Son of God and will have come to the age of the perfect Man, the full measure of the stature of Christ—it is toward this that tends the life of the mystical body.

I exhort you, therefore, I, the prisoner of the Lord, to walk worthily of the calling wherewith ye were called, with all humility and meekness, with long suffering, bearing one with another in charity, careful to keep the unity of the Spirit in the bond of peace : one Body and one Spirit, as also ye were called in one hope, that of your calling : one Lord, one faith, one baptism : one God and Father of all, who is above all and throughout all and in all.

But to every one of us is given grace according to the measure of Christ's bestowing. Wherefore it is said :

Ascending on high he led captives into captivity,
He gave gifts to men.[2]

Now this phrase, "he ascended," what does it mean but that he had

---

[1] Cf. above, p. 77.   [2] Ps. lxviii. (lxvii.) 18.

also descended into the lower parts of the earth. He that descended, the same is also he that ascended above all the heavens, that he might fill all things with his presence. And himself " gave " some as apostles, some as prophets, some as evangelists, some as shepherds and teachers, for the perfecting of the saints in the work of ministry, unto the build-ing up of the body of Christ, till we all attain to the unity of the faith and of the full knowledge of the Son of God, to the perfect man, to the full measure of the stature of Christ.

Thus we shall be no longer children, nor tossed on the waves and carried around by every wind of doctrine, through the trickery of men crafty in devising error. Rather we shall hold the truth in charity, and grow in all things into him who is the head, Christ. From him the whole body, welded and compacted together by means of that which every joint supplieth, part working with part—from him the body deriveth its increase, unto the building up of itself in charity. [Ephes. iv. 1–16.]

Christ is head of the body, the Church. [Colos. i. 18.]

And whereas ye were at one time estranged and at enmity of mind through your evil deeds, yet now Christ hath reconciled you by the body of his flesh through his death, so as to present you holy and blame-less and irreproachable in his sight, if only ye hold by the faith, well-grounded and steadfast, without swerving from the hope of the glad tidings which ye have heard, which hath been preached to every creature under heaven, of which I, Paul, am become a minister. [Colos. i. 21–23.]

The Old Covenant was entered into in fear. The New Cove-nant, in grace ; and the mystical body of Christ already forms and builds, in its earthly pilgrimage and its crucified life, and in the darkness of faith, the city of the living God, the heavenly Jerusalem " which is to come " [Heb. xiii. 14].

Ye have not approached unto a material mountain " which burneth with fire, unto gloom and darkness and storm-wind, unto clang of trumpet, and sound of words " [1]—whereat the listeners prayed that no word more be spoken to them, for they could not bear the command, " If even a beast touch the mountain, it shall be stoned." Yea, so dreadful was the scene that Moses said, " I am full of fear and tremble." Rather ye have approached unto Mount Sion, and the city of the living God, the heavenly Jerusalem, to the myriads of angels, to the festal

---

[1] Cf. Exod. xix. 12–16 ; Deut. iv. 11–12 ; v. 24–27 ; ix. 19.

gathering and assemblage of the firstborn registered in heaven, to God the judge of all, to the spirits of the just made perfect, to Jesus the Mediator of the New Testament, and to that blood of sprinkling which speaketh better than Abel's. [Heb. xii. 18–24.]

The Continued Redemption

How can the work that the mystical body has to accomplish here below be other than the very work for which Christ came ? It is the work of redemption continued in time, by the preaching of truth, and by the fulfilment, through all ages, of " what is lacking to the sufferings of the Saviour "—not indeed as to merits, for He has paid by His blood once for all and for all men, but as to the application of the merits of Christ by means of the communion of saints to the human generations and to those who, sitting in the shadow of death, await their redemption.

To you this hath been granted on Christ's behalf, not only to believe in him but also to suffer for him. [Philip. i. 29.]

Let that mind be in you, which was also in Christ Jesus. For he, though he was by nature God . . . humbled himself by obedience unto death, yea unto death upon a cross. [Philip. ii. 5, 8.]

Now I rejoice in my sufferings on your behalf, and make up in my flesh what is lacking to the sufferings of Christ, on behalf of his body, which is the Church, whereof I am become a minister.

Such is indeed the commission of God given me in your regard, to utter the full word of God touching the mystery which hath been made manifest to his saints, to whom God hath willed to make known what is the wealth of the glory of this mystery for the gentiles, which is Christ within you, your hope of glory. Him do we proclaim, admonishing every man and teaching every man with all wisdom, that we may present every man perfect in Christ. For this I labour and struggle, with the help of that divine energy which worketh powerfully in me. [Colos. i. 24–29.]

Marriage

Marriage does not depend only on the natural law ; it is also a sacrament. The union of the two spouses is the sign or the emblem of the union of Christ and the Church ; for the

Church has her personality—more real and more profound than the "moral personality" of purely human "perfect societies"; it is because the Church has a personality that she has a voice and she cries to the Lord Jesus : Come ! "And the Spirit and the Spouse say : Come ! " [Apoc. xxii. 17]. The Church and Christ are two in the same flesh, which is human nature. The Church is a spouse, and a spouse who has her very being, her soul and her life from the Bridegroom ; and it is by this double reason that she is the body of Christ ; " bone of my bones and flesh of my flesh " [Gen. ii. 23]. As a sign of that union, the sacrament of matrimony enables man and woman in their own union to realize a participation in that union. That is why Christian marriage carries the requirements and refinements of the natural law to a point of perfection which can only find its fulfilment by and in grace.

Wives [be subject] to your husbands, as to the Lord, because the husband is the head of the wife, as Christ too is the head of the Church, himself being the saviour of the body. Well, then, as the Church is subject to Christ, so also should wives be to their husbands in everything.

Husbands, love your wives, as Christ also loved the Church and delivered himself up for her, that he might sanctify her, purifying her in the bath of water by means of the word, and that he might present her to himself a glorious Church, not having spot or wrinkle or any such thing, but holy and without blemish. Even thus ought husbands to love their wives as their own bodies. He that loveth his own wife loveth himself. Surely no man ever hated his own flesh, nay, he doth nourish and cherish it, even as Christ the Church ; because we are members of his body. " For this shall man leave father and mother, and shall cleave to his wife, and the two shall come to be one flesh." [1] This mystery is great—I mean in regard to the Church. However, let each of you, also, love his wife even as himself ; and let the wife reverence her husband. [Ephes. v. 22-23.]

This passage from the Epistle to the Ephesians shows that in Paul's eyes marriage is above all the mystery of the indissoluble union—realized through a love which divine charity penetrates, and at once spiritual and carnal and fruitful—between two human persons. In the first Epistle to the Corinthians he

[1] Gen. ii. 24.

speaks from the point of view of practical morals which was made necessary by the questions put to him : if the state of chastity is in itself superior to the married state, what are we to say to those who, lacking any higher motive, dare not choose the former state because the desires of the flesh seem to them to be too strong in them ? In Paul's answers, this aspect of the question becomes, then, of the first importance also, but it would be a grave mistake to believe that all Paul's thought on marriage amounts to seeing in it a remedy for concupiscence.

Now concerning the matters whereof ye wrote ; it is good for a man not to touch woman. Yet, for fear of impurity, let each man have his own wife, and let each woman have her own husband. Let the husband render to his wife her due, and likewise the wife to her husband. The wife hath not control of her own body in this matter, but the husband ; the husband likewise hath not control of his own body, but the wife. Deprive not one another of your due, unless it be by consent for a time, that you may devote yourselves to prayer and then be together again, lest Satan use your lack of self-control to tempt you. But this I say by way of concession, not by way of command. I wish all men to be as myself ; nevertheless, each hath his own gift from God, one in this way, and one in that.

Then, to the unmarried and to the widows I say, it is good for them if they remain even as I. But if they have not self-control, let them marry ; it is better to marry than to be on fire. To the married I give this charge nay, not I, but the Lord—that a wife depart not from her husband (but if she have departed, let her remain unmarried, or be reconciled to her husband), and that a husband put not away his wife.

But to the rest, it is I who speak, not the Lord : If any brother hath an unbelieving wife, and she is content to live with him, let him not put her away. And the wife that hath an unbelieving husband, who is content to live with her, let her not put away her husband. For the unbelieving husband is sanctified in the wife, and the unbelieving wife is sanctified in the brother. Else were your children 'unclean' ; whereas now they are holy. (But if the unbeliever depart, let him depart ; the brother or the sister is under no bondage in such cases, but God hath called you unto peace.) For how knowest thou, O wife, but what thou shalt save thy husband ? Or how knowest thou, O husband, but what thou shalt save thy wife ? [1 Cor. vii. 1-16.]

The term "Pauline privilege" has been applied to the permission herein granted by the Apostle to that one of the two spouses who is a Christian to leave the other if the other, not a Christian, refuses cohabitation or makes it morally impossible, and the permission for the former to contract a second marriage which, if itself, annuls the first.

The expectation of the *parousia* (the second coming of the Saviour), so lively in the hearts of Christians of apostolic times, gives its own special emotional shade to Paul's teaching on the subject of the state of virginity. But that teaching remains substantially independent of this shade, and Paul's realistic remarks are of value in themselves and for any age. They further in no sense tend, of themselves, to make of the married state a "state of imperfection," since, by the very power of the sacrament, this state is in itself a holy state. But they do show that with regard to the service of the Lord and of progress toward perfection, marriage is a difficult state, which bears with it afflictions of the flesh, embarrassments and complications not involved in the state of virginity.

Now concerning virgins I have no commandment of the Lord, but I speak my mind, as one by the mercy of the Lord rendered trustworthy. I think therefore that this state is good on account of the present distress—that it is good for a man so to be. Art thou bound to a wife? Seek not to be loosed. Art thou not so bound? Seek not a wife. But if thou marry, thou hast not sinned ; and if a virgin marry, she hath not sinned. Yet such as marry shall have affliction in the flesh ; but I spare you.

But this I say, brethren, the time is short : henceforth let those that have wives be as having them not, and those that weep as weeping not, and those that rejoice as rejoicing not, and those that buy as possessing not, and those that use the world as not using it to the full. For the world as we see it is passing away. My desire is to have you free from care. He that is unmarried hath a care for the things of the Lord, how he may please the Lord ; but he that is married hath a care for the things of the world, how he may please his wife, and he is drawn different ways. So also the unmarried woman and the virgin hath a care for the things of the Lord, that she may be holy both in body and soul, whilst the married woman hath a care for the things of the world, how she may please her husband. Now this I say for your own profit, not that I may cast a snare upon you, but

8

for the sake of seemly and devoted and undistracted service of the Lord. [1 Cor. vii. 25-35.]

As for himself, Paul has an open distrust of women, and he would doubtless have felt no sympathy for what is to-day called the claims of feminism (some of which claims were perhaps already in the mind of the Corinthian ladies of his day). These personal dispositions to a certain extent colour the form in which he states truths which it is important for us to perceive in their essential meaning ; and also warns us to disengage the phrases he uses from the special connotations which applied in his environment and times.

If the equal dignity, in man and in woman, of the spiritual soul and of the human person admits of a profound functional diversity, and if in marriage man has primacy with regard to authority (the woman having for her part primacy with regard to love, and being well aware of it) it would be completely to distort Saint Paul's views on this subject to find in them I know not what essential difference on an intellectual or moral level, for which reason might be sought in biology and on which it might be desired to establish a sociological rule. Their meaning is a very high metaphysical meaning. They relate to the metaphysical finalities inscribed in nature, and to the fact that womanhood as such is directed toward man, and hence toward love, wherein it finds its fulfilment, whereas the masculine nature as such is directed toward the operation of the reason (that is to say, in the supernatural order, toward the Incarnate Word) and hence toward authority over nature, in which it finds its fulfilment.

This I would have you know, that the head of every man is Christ, and the head of the woman is the man, and the head of Christ is God. [1 Cor. xi. 3.]

A man ought not to cover his head, because man is the image and glory of God ; but woman is the glory of man. For man is not from woman, but woman from man ; for man was not created for the sake of woman, but woman for the sake of man. . . .

Yet, in the Lord, neither is woman a being independent of man nor man a being independent of woman. For as woman is from man, so man is through woman ; yea, and all things are from God.

Judge for yourselves; is it seemly that a woman pray to God uncovered? [1 Cor. xi. 7–9; 11–13.]

Let women be silent in the churches, for it is not allowed them to speak in public; but let them be submissive, as also saith the Law. If they would seek some information, let them ask their own husbands at home. [1 Cor. xiv. 34–35.]

For Adam was first formed, then Eve; and it was not Adam who was deceived, but the woman who being deluded fell into transgression. Nevertheless, women shall be saved through child-bearing, if they abide in faith and charity and holiness, with self-control. [1 Tim. ii. 13–15.]

It is because Adam had a natural primacy of authority that his sin in consenting was more grave than the sin of Eve in letting herself be deceived. The punishment inflicted on man and woman implies that they will be saved if the one accept the law of working the earth by the sweat of his brow, and the other the law of childbirth in suffering—unless they should be called to a higher vocation, with which Paul deals in the first Epistle to the Corinthians, for the one part when speaking of the ministry of the Gospel (" the Lord directed those who proclaim the Gospel to live by the Gospel," ix. 14), for the other part when speaking of virginity (vii).

The Temporal Order

Paul came to evangelize and preach the Kingdom of God, not to reform temporal society. He does not deal directly with the temporal order; he deals with it only in relation to the Kingdom of God. But by this very fact, his teaching touches upon certain very high principles of that order.

He wrote in the days of Nero. His doctrine regarding the respect owing in conscience to temporal authority, a respect of which the value as a moral obligation has its immediate foundation in the author of nature, is therefore all the more significant.

Let every soul be subject to the higher authorities. There is no authority that is not from God, and the existing authorities are appointed by God. Wherefore he that opposeth the authorities resisteth

the ordinance of God ; and they that resist shall bring upon themselves
a judgment. For the rulers are a cause of fear ; not to the good work,
but to the bad. Dost thou wish not to fear the authorities ? Do what
is good, and thou shalt have praise from them ; for they are God's
ministers to thee unto good. But if thou do what is evil, then be afraid,
for they bear not the sword in vain ; they are still God's ministers, to
inflict his wrathful vengeance upon him that doth wrong. Therefore
one must needs be subject, not merely for fear of the wrath, but also
for conscience' sake. And it is for this reason, too, that ye pay them
taxes ; for they are the functionaries of God in devoting themselves to
this very work. Render to all their due, tribute to whom tribute is
due, taxes to whom taxes are due, fear to whom fear is due, honour to
whom honour is due. [Rom. xiii. 1-7.]

To whatever use, good or bad, governors put their authority,
it remains founded in God and participating in a sense in the
mystery of Christ's kingship, and hence it requires of us
obedience in conscience. Excepting, of course, if the governor
command the accomplishment of an act contrary to the law
of God : then one must resist, according to the answer given
by the Apostles Peter and John to the Sandehrin, " Judge ye,
whether it be right before God to hearken to you rather than
to God " [Acts iv. 19]. Theologians were later to explain
that an unjust law betrays the essence of the law, and does not
bind in conscience. (Which follows from the very principles
of St. Paul ; since the prince, being " God's minister," obviously
cannot act in this quality when commanding anything unjust.) They would distinguish as well between legitimate and
illegitimate power. (To the latter we are bound in obedience
only to the extent that disobedience would carry with it greater
evils for the community, not because it can have in itself the
right to be obeyed.)

The leaven of the Gospels, once introduced into the mass,
will work upon the world from within, and will prompt, in
the long run, changes in the temporal order itself. It is precisely
for this reason that the preacher of the Gospel as such need not
trouble to improve things in the temporal community ; he
leaves that to others. His essential task is to supply a pure
leaven for life eternal. Paul accomplished more toward the

abolition of slavery by teaching the essential equality before God of slave and master than if he had made a frontal attack on the juridical institutions of his day. He takes temporal situations as they exist at the time he is speaking. And he teaches Christians to apply thereto the spirit of the New Law.

Only, as the Lord hath allotted to each, as God hath called each, so let him continue to walk : such is my ruling in all the churches. Was any man called in circumcision ? Let him not undo it. Hath any been called in uncircumcision ? Let him not be circumcised. Circumcision is nothing and uncircumcision is nothing ; but the keeping of the commandments of God is all in all. Let each abide in the condition wherein the call found him. Wast thou a slave when called ? Let it not trouble thee ; though if thou canst become free, rather choose that. For the slave that hath been called in the Lord is a freedman of the Lord, and likewise the free man that hath been called is a slave of Christ. Ye have been bought at a price ; do not become slaves of men. In what condition each was called, brethren, therein let him remain with God. [I Cor. vii. 17-24.]

Wives, be subject to your husbands, as it behoveth in the Lord.

Husbands, love your wives and be not bitter towards them.

Children, obey your parents in all things, for this is well-pleasing in the Lord.

Fathers, do not irritate your children, that they may not lose heart.

Slaves, obey in all things your masters according to the flesh, not with eye-service, to please men, but in singleness of heart, fearing the Lord. Whatever ye do, work at it from your soul, as for the Lord and not for men, knowing that from the Lord ye shall receive the inheritance as reward. Be ye slaves of the Lord Christ. For he that dealeth wrongfully shall reap the fruit of his wrongdoing, and with God there is no respect of persons.

Masters, be just and fair to your slaves, knowing that ye too have a master in heaven. [Colos. iii. 18-25 ; iv. 1.]

Slaves, obey your masters according to the flesh as Christ, with fear and trembling, in singleness of heart, not with eye-service to please men, but as slaves of Christ, doing the will of God from your soul, serving with good will as to the Lord and not to men : for ye know that whatever good thing each one doth, the same shall he receive again from the Lord, be he slave or free.

And do ye, masters, act in the same way towards them, and forbear threatening, knowing that both ye and they have a master in heaven, and that with him there is no respect of persons. [Ephes. vi. 5-9.]

The brief epistle to Philemon, full as it is of kindliness and Christian humanism, is good evidence at once of Paul's sweetness of heart and of the new dignity in which Christianity clothed the slave. Philemon was an eminent member of the church of Colossae ; it seems that his slave Onesimus had left him, perhaps after having committed some trespass ; the slave had come to find Paul at Rome, where Paul baptized him. Paul pleads his case with Philemon, to whom he sends back, together with the epistle in question, this Onesimus (" useful " in Greek), on whose name he humorously plays. In such a case a master could inflict terrible punishments, going even as far as crucifixion. Philemon, being a Christian, would not have shown himself so cruel ; but what Paul asks of him is to receive Onesimus as Paul's very " heart," and as a " well beloved brother."

And so, though I have in Christ boldness in abundance to charge thee with what is fitting, for charity's sake I rather plead as, what I am, Paul, an old man, and now besides a prisoner for Christ Jesus. I plead with thee for this my child, whom I have begotten in my bondage, Onesimus, a man once worthless to thee, but now of great worth, to thee as well as to me. Him have I sent back to thee in his own person, that is my very heart. I could have wished to keep him with me, that on thy behalf he might minister to me in my bonds for the gospel. But I have determined to do nothing without thy consent, that thy good deed may not come of compulsion but of thy free-will.

Perhaps for this very reason he hath been separated from thee for a time, that thou mayest receive him as thine for ever, no longer as a slave, but as better than a slave, a beloved brother, especially to me, but how much more to thee, both in the flesh and in the Lord. If then thou dost hold me thine in fellowship, receive him as thou wouldst myself. And if he hath wronged thee in any way, or oweth aught to thee, charge it to me. I, Paul, write it with mine own hand, I will repay thee—to say naught of thine owing me thy very self. Yea, brother, let me have this profit from thee in the Lord ; cheer my heart in Christ.

I write to thee with confidence in thy compliance, knowing that thou wilt do even more than I say. And furthermore, get ready accommodation for me ; for I hope that through your prayers I shall be granted to you. [Philem. 8-22.]

Another point which in Paul's teaching touches upon the temporal order is that wherein the law of work is prescribed for all. "If any man will not work, neither let him eat." By this formula, which was perhaps a Jewish aphorism, Paul does not mean to require everyone to do manual labour, or, even more generally, labour economically productive. But the word work can be taken in a much broader sense, including everything which redounds from man's activity to useful service for the community (even the altogether inward activities which suit a state of life dedicated to contemplation and prayer). In that sense each man is expected, in accordance with his condition, his gifts, his possibilities to play his personal part in the burdens of the community.

Yourselves know how ye ought to imitate us, in that we were not disorderly whilst with you, neither did we take food unearned at any man's hand, but we worked night and day in toil and struggle, that we might not burden any of you ; not that we have not the right so to do, but we wished to furnish in ourselves a pattern for you to imitate. For indeed when we were with you, these were our instructions— If any man will not work, neither let him eat. For we hear of some among you who are disorderly, doing no work but interfering with others ; such as these we charge and exhort in the Lord Jesus Christ that they work peacefully and earn the food they eat. [2 Thes. iii. 7-12.]

And finally what Paul says about the love of money, which is the "root of all evils," doubtless principally concerns the spiritual evils arising therefrom, but it applies also to the disorders and evils from which suffers the earthly community.

They who desire to be rich fall into the temptation and a snare, and into many senseless and hurtful lusts, which plunge men into destruction and perdition. For the love of money is the root of all evils, and some that have been eager for it have been led astray from the faith, and have pierced themselves with many pangs. [1 Tim. vi. 9-10.]

The Resurrection

Now I make known to you again, brethren, the gospel which I preached to you, which also ye received, wherein indeed ye stand, through which ye are being saved ; recalling to you in what terms I preached it to you, if ye hold fast thereto—unless ye have believed to no purpose. For I have delivered to you before all else, what I also had received, that Christ died for our sins according to the scriptures, and that he was buried, and that he rose on the third day according to the scriptures ; and that he appeared to Cephas [Peter], and then to the twelve.[1] After that he appeared to more than five hundred brethren at once, most of whom still survive, though some have fallen asleep. After that he appeared to James, and then to all the apostles. Last of all, as to one born out of due time, he appeared also to me. For I am the least of the apostles, and am not worthy to be called an apostle, because I persecuted the church of God. But by the grace of God I am what I am, and the grace he gave me hath not been fruitless ; nay, I have laboured more than all of them, yet not I, but the grace of God with me. Whether therefore I or they, so we preach, and so ye have believed.

Now if Christ is preached as risen from the dead, how say some among you that there is no resurrection of the dead ? If there is no resurrection of the dead, neither is Christ risen ; and if Christ is not risen, vain truly is our preaching, vain too your faith. Yea, and we are found to be false witnesses concerning God, because we have witnessed of God that he raised Christ—whom he did not raise, if after all the dead do not rise. For if the dead do not rise, neither is Christ risen ; and if Christ is not risen, your faith is futile, ye are still in your sins. Those, too, who have fallen asleep in Christ have after all perished. If it be in view of this life alone that we have set our hopes in Christ, we are more to be pitied than all men.

But, in truth, Christ is risen from the dead, the firstfruits of them that sleep. For since by a man came death, by a man also cometh resurrection from the dead. For as in Adam all die, so in Christ all shall be made to live. But each in his own order : Christ the firstfruits, then they that are Christ's shall rise, at his coming ; then shall be the end, when he shall surrender the kingdom to God the Father, when he shall have brought to nought all other rule and all other authority and power. For he must reign until the Father " hath put all his enemies under his feet." [2] The last enemy to be brought to nought is death : for [the Father] " hath subjected *all* things beneath his feet." [3] (Now, when it is said that *all* things are subject, he of course is excepted who hath subjected all things to him.) And when all things shall be subject to him, then shall the Son himself be subject to the Father who subjected all things to him, that God may be all in all. [1 Cor. xv. 1-28.]

---

[1] Judas was dead, but " the twelve " had come to be the regular term ; cf. John xx. 24.

[2] Ps. cx. (cix.) 1. [3] Ps. viii. 6.

Thus the mission that Christ has to accomplish in time is to subdue all things—and all His enemies, that is to say all those forces which impede the grace of regeneration—to His law and His power, which are not the law and power of any political constraint, but the supernatural law and power of redemption by His blood, until at the very end death itself is subdued. Then, at the end of time, He will offer Himself, as the perfect Man, and with Him, His universal conquest, to the Father Who sent Him.

Why are we, too, in jeopardy every hour? Yea, by that boasting in you, brethren, which is mine in Christ Jesus our Lord, I die daily. If with human prospects I have fought with wild beasts [1] at Ephesus, what doth it profit me? If the dead do not rise, "let us eat and drink, for to-morrow we die." [2] Be not deceived : "Evil company doth corrupt good manners." [3] Rouse yourselves to righteousness, and sin not ; for some lack knowledge of God. I speak thus to shame you.

But some one will say, "How do the dead rise? And with what manner of body are they coming?" Senseless man ! What thou sowest thyself is not brought to life unless it die, and when thou sowest, thou sowest not the body that shall be, but a bare grain—of wheat, for example, or of some other kind ; but God giveth it a body as he hath determined, and to each seed a body of its own.

Not all flesh is the same flesh, but there is one flesh belonging to men, another flesh to beasts, another flesh to birds, another to fish. And there are heavenly bodies, and earthly bodies ; but the glory of the heavenly is different from that of the earthly. There is the glory of the sun, and the glory of the moon, and the glory of the stars ; for star differeth from star in glory. And so it is with the resurrection of the dead. What is shown in corruption doth rise in incorruption ; what is sown in dishonour doth rise in glory ; what is sown in weakness doth rise in power ; what is sown a natural body doth rise a spiritual body.

If there is a natural body, there is also a spiritual body. Even so it is written, the first man Adam became "a living soul" [4] : the last Adam [Jesus-Christ] became a life-giving spirit. But it is not the spiritual which is first, but the natural, and then the spiritual. The first man was from the earth, earthly ; the second man is from heaven. As was the earthly man, such are the earthly ; and as is the heavenly man,

---

[1] Doubtless this is intended as metaphorical.
[2] Isa. xxii. 13.
[3] A line from *Thais*. a lost comedy by Menander.
[4] Gen. ii. 7.

such are the heavenly. And even as we have borne the likeness of the
earthly, so let us bear the likeness of the heavenly.

Now this I say, brethren, that flesh and blood cannot inherit the
kingdom of God, neither doth corruption inherit incorruption. Behold,
I tell you a mystery : we shall not all fall asleep, but we shall all be
changed, in a moment, in the twinkling of an eye, at the sound of the
last trumpet. For the trumpet shall sound, and the dead shall rise
incorruptible, and we shall be changed. For this corruptible body
must needs put on incorruption, and this mortal body immortality.
And when this mortal body shall have put on immortality, then shall
come to pass the word which is written,

> Death is swallowed up in victory !
> O Death, where is thy victory ?
> O Death, where is thy sting ? [1]
>
>   [1 Cor. xv. 30-55.]

" We shall not fall asleep, but we shall all be changed."
This statement refers to the just. Those who find themselves
on earth at the last day will have their bodies glorified without
having to endure death. As for the men whom the sounding
of the last trumpet will find wilful in the refusal of grace,
they will suffer the law of death, and the resurrection of their
bodies will not be a glorious transfiguration, by the power of
the resurrection in Christ, but the seal of their chastisement.

Now would we not have you ignorant, brethren, touching them
that sleep, that ye grieve not, even as the rest who have no hope. For
as we believe that Jesus died and rose again, God will likewise bring
with Jesus those who have fallen asleep through him. For this we tell
you as the Lord's word, that we who live, who survive until the Lord's
coming, shall not precede them that are fallen asleep. For the Lord
himself at a signal—the voice of the archangel and the trumpet of God
—shall come down from heaven ; and the dead in Christ shall rise
first. Thereupon we the living, who survive, shall together with them
be caught upon the clouds to meet the Lord in the air, and thus we
shall be ever with the Lord. Comfort ye one another therefore with
these words. [1 Thes. iv. 13-18.]

" We who survive." That is to say ourselves if we are
among those who will survive. The phrase does not mean
that Paul was certain of the proximity of the last days.

---

[1] Isa. xxv. 8 ; Hos. xiii. 14.

The Last Days

Touching the times and the seasons, brethren, ye need not any written instructions, for yourselves know well that the day of the Lord cometh as a thief in the night. For when they are saying, Peace and safety, even then is ruin upon them, sudden as the birth-pang upon the woman with child, and they shall not escape. [1 Thes. v. 1–3.]

This text clearly shows that Paul shared the general ignorance on the subject of the time when will come the " day of the Lord." The expectation of Jesus returning here below was lively and ardent in the primitive Church, and it is the very intensity of this desire, it was no positive teaching or no belief held as a point of faith, which led to the expectation of the second coming as something imminent.

But know this, that in the last days grievous times will set in. For men will be selfish, covetous, boastful, haughty, railers, disobedient to parents, ungrateful, unholy, unloving, implacable, slanderers, dissolute, unbridled, no lovers of good, treacherous, headstrong, besotted with pride, lovers of pleasure rather than of God, with a semblance of piety, but repudiating the living force thereof. [2 Tim. iii. 1–5.]

Such are the men whom Timothy should ward off, for there are always such men. But in the last days they will swarm.

Such as these do thou ward off. For of these are they that make their way into houses, and take captive silly women who are laden with sins and led about by manifold lusts, yea, ever learning and never able to come to the knowledge of truth. But as Jannes and Jambres withstood Moses, so do these men withstand the truth, being depraved in mind, and reprobate in regard to faith. Nevertheless they will not make further progress, for their folly will be quite clear to all, as was that of the men aforesaid. [2 Tim. iii. 5–9.]

" Jannes and Jambres " were in the Jewish tradition the names of the principal magicians of Pharaoh.

There will come a time when men will not endure the sound doctrine, but following their own lusts will keep up to themselves teachers, to tickle their ears, and while refusing to listen to the truth, they will turn aside unto fables. [2 Tim. iv. 3-4.]

Saint Paul describes the Antichrist as ὁ ἄνομος, the lawless. No law will exist for him, except his will to power. As has been pointed out by Prat, the picture Paul paints of him is made up of allusions to ancient texts. He will exalt himself against all that which is called God or is venerated, as it has been said of Antiochus Epiphanes. He will palm himself off as God and will wish to be treated as God, like the prince of Tyre in Ezechiel and the king of Babylon in Isaiah. He will take his seat in the very temple of God, like the abomination of desolation foretold by Daniel. Here are " symbols that can be realized in accordance with a law of proportion which escapes us," although the present course of the history of the world already permits certain forebodings.

Now we beseech you, brethren, touching the coming of our Lord Jesus Christ and our being gathered together unto him, that ye be not readily shaken out of your right mind nor kept in alarm—whether by spirit-utterance or by discourse or by a letter purporting to be from us—as though the day of the Lord were upon us. Let no man in any way beguile you ; for unless the apostasy first come to pass, and there be revealed the man of lawlessness, the son of perdition, who shall oppose and exalt himself against all that is called God or is venerated, even to the seating himself in God's sanctuary and giving himself out as God—but do ye not remember that while I was still with you I used to tell you these things ? And now ye know what keepeth him back, to the end he may be revealed in his own season. For the mystery of lawlessness is already at work ; only let him be taken out of the way who now keepeth him back, and then shall the lawless one be revealed, whom the Lord Jesus shall slay with the breath of his mouth and bring to nought by the manifestation of his coming. But the other's coming is through Satan's working attended by every kind of feat and sign and lying-wonder, and by every seduction to evil for them that are perishing, because they have not entertained the love of the truth unto their salvation. And therefore God sendeth them a working of error, that they should believe that lie, in order that all may be judged that have not believed the truth, but have resolved upon unrighteousness. [2 Thes. ii. 1-11.]

" The mystery of lawlessness is already at work." There

will be many antichrists up until the last, who will deserve the name in its utter fulness. Who is it Paul means to indicate by the power which keeps back until the appointed hour the mystery of iniquity—" him who now keepeth back " ? Saint Augustine and Thomas Aquinas confess that they can make nothing out of it. Others, less cautious, have advanced all kinds of hypotheses on this subject. Prat, pointing out that Saint Paul stays on the ground of Jewish and Christian eschatology, thinks that the opponent of the man of lawlessness must be the chief of the people of God, Michael at the head of his angels. The view of Tertullian, of Saint Jerome, of Saint John Chrysostom, according to whom the Antagonist of Antichrist was the Roman Empire, has clearly been shown wrong by history. The pagan empire of Nero and Diocletian had been the enemy of the Gospel, the very seat of the mystery of iniquity. And this is true of every pagan empire and of any pagan politics, in which it is an illusion to seek the antagonist of the man of iniquity. The Roman Empire of the days of Saint Jerome and Saint John Chrysostom was a new patch sewn on to a worn and dirty cloth.

Still one can ask oneself whether another hypothesis could not be formulated, taking historical relativity more into account. The antagonist of the Antichrist might be the truly human heritage and the truly human pattern of temporal civilization (to the extent that these had emerged in Rome, something of them continued still in the decadent Empire)—and principally the heritage and the pattern of Christian civilization : of that Christendom which was built up, with elements both good and bad, by the Middle Ages, and which long since had little by little been crumbling, and which, moreover, according to Paul's teaching on the mystery of Israel, will flower again some day, under new forms, like a resurrection for the world.

The text from the Second Epistle to the Thessalonians does not necessarily suggest that the moment when the Lord Jesus will put to death the man of iniquity " with the breath of his mouth " and will annihilate him " by the manifestation of his coming " will coincide with the second coming itself. These words may indicate an extraordinary intervention of the power of Christ, which will be like an effluence visible to all eyes [1] and a manifestation before the time of this future event.[2]

[1] " The first flush of dawn," says Filion [2 Thes. ii. 8].

[2] Some authors think that a separation must be made between the two actions expressed in the words " to slay with the breath of his mouth " and " to bring to naught by the manifestation of his coming." Father Allo writes to this effect : " Christ will struggle against him and will conquer him perhaps at a single blow, but also perhaps at the end of a period of struggles, by means of the weapons of His word. Finally He will destroy him utterly with the *parousia* of Christ appearing to judge the living and the dead." (Apocalypse of Saint John, Introduction, p. cxix.) The separation thus suggested seems to me difficult to justify. On the other hand, I think that the " manifestation of his coming " does not indicate the last judgment itself, but the brilliance thereof before the event, and means that the Saviour will annihilate the Antichrist " by the triumph of His Gospel over all heresies and by the establishment of His Church over all nations." Father Gallois, *Apocalypse of Saint John*, p. 80 ; cf. Father Fortuné de la Vallette, *Apocalypse of Saint John, Revue de l'Université d'Ottawa*, July–October, 1938, to January–April, 1939.

CHAPTER VIII

THE NEW MAN

The Gift of God

GOD, WHEN HE CREATED THE WORLD AND NATURE, ABOVE
all planned—a thing in the order of grace and glory,
and surpassing the whole order of nature and the world
—to give Himself for those He loves, and to raise them up
in order that they might participate in His own life in Christ
the Redeemer, in Whom all things must be reconciled and
together borne on high.

Blessed be the God and Father of our Lord Jesus Christ, who hath
blessed us with every spiritual blessing on high in Christ. Yea, in
him he singled us out before the foundation of the world, that we might
be holy and blameless in his sight. In love he predestined us to be
adopted as his sons through Jesus Christ, according to the good pleasure
of his will, unto the praise of the glory of his grace, wherewith he
hath made us gracious in the Well-beloved. In him we have redemption
through his blood, the forgiveness of our transgressions, according
to the riches of his grace. For God hath given us abundance thereof,
together with full wisdom and discernment, in that he hath made
known to us the secret of his purpose according to his good pleasure.
It was the purpose of his good pleasure in him—a dispensation to be
realized in the fulness of time—to bring all things to a head in Christ,
both the things in the heavens and the things upon the earth.
In him we also have come to have our portion, having been predestined, in the purpose of him that worketh all things according
to the council of his will, ourselves to further the praise of his glory,
as having been the first to hope in Christ. In him are ye too, who have
heard the word of truth, the glad tidings of your salvation. For ye
have believed therein, and have been sealed with the Holy Spirit of
the promise, who is the earnest of our inheritance, unto redemption
as the chosen people, unto praise of his glory. [Ephes. i. 3–14.]

God loves all men and wills that all be saved.

God our Saviour willeth all men to be saved and to come to knowledge of truth. [1 Tim. ii. 4.]

119

There is therefore no predestination to perdition. But there is a predestination to glory, since it is by virtue of His eternal love, which precedes all merit on the creature's part, that God saves all those who do not of themselves cut themselves off from His love, and whom he knows from all eternity, and whom the proveniences of His grace have abundantly filled.

Those whom he hath foreknown, them he hath predestined to bear a nature in the image of his Son's, that he should be first-born among many brethren. And those whom he hath predestined, them he hath also called : and those whom he hath called, them He hath also justified, and those whom he hath justified, them he hath also glorified. [Rom. viii. 29–39.]

Those who are lost, are lost through their own fault, because they strip themselves of the gift of God. Those who are saved are saved by the grace of God, Who gives them the will and the performance. They have nothing which they have not received. It is not they who have singled themselves out by their merits for life eternal, it is the saving will of God which from the outset and before the constitution of the world has willed that life to them : those who are loved up to the end and do not say No. Whereas those who are lost have singled themselves out for punishment, because they have made vain in themselves the proffered gift.

The principal text wherein Paul sets forth his teaching on this subject is to be found in the Epistle to the Romans in a context which relates to the vocation of Israel and the temporary rejection thereof. The gentiles who were waiting in the shadow of death are called to the faith, while the holy nation, the priestly race, the house of Jehovah is disinherited. How did the people to which all was promised stumble over the stumbling-block ? How is this unheard-of catastrophe, which God turns to the salvation of the gentiles and which permits His Church to be that which He wished it should be, to be given its meaning with reference to divine ways and without man's having a right to complain at them ? Paul replies in accordance with the great unshatterable answer of faith, calling up, as did God Himself in the Book of Job, the sublimity and the freedom or the All-Powerful before Whom all human mouths are closed.

It is thus in thinking at first of the destiny of a people in this world, that he lifts himself up to considerations which the perspective wherein he is situated permits us to apply as well, in a certain manner, to the eternal destiny of souls. And he expresses these ideas in Semitic style, according to which, when he would say that God loved Esau less than Jacob, Malachy writes : " I have loved Jacob and Esau have I hated." When, in connection with the Jews who betray their vocation here below, Paul recalls a phrase in Exodus [vii. 3] and says that God has " hardened " Pharaoh, we must remember that elsewhere the Scripture equivalently says that " Pharaoh hardened his heart " [Exod. viii. 28]. The hardening of the heart does not come from God but trom the failing creature. This is even more the case if we turn from the order of worldly events to the order of eternal life. God wishes to save Pharaoh like the rest of mankind, and gives him sufficient means thereto. It is Pharaoh who, rejecting this help, thereby himself hardens himself, God permitting or suffering this, not willing it.

Mercy does not work against justice, but above it. God is just, and His grace quits only him who first withdraws himself from it. But God is merciful to whomsoever He will be, and His pity goes out to whomsoever He will have it go : that is the privilege of His freedom. Moses was chosen from among the other children of Israel, not from his merits, but because it pleased God that Moses *should be*, for the mission which it pleased Him to give him, and which he would freely and meritoriously fulfil under the divine inflowing. So also, with regard to eternal life, it is not from man's effort, it is from the free mercy of God that comes the gift of grace—offered to all men and, of their own initiative, not accepted by some. If Pharaoh appeared in human history with those special predispositions which, like each of us, he owed to his burden of heredity, and with that heart which freely hardened itself in the sight of God, Who tolerated it, it was in order that the power of God should be made better manifest in the world. So He shows mercy to whomsoever He will, and He lets harden himself whoever will. God holds the peoples in His hand,

and from the same human mass He draws forth shapes which, with regard to their collective temporal destinies, are vessels of honour or vessels of shame. And if He endures with great patience vessels of wrath which he had shaped for the good, and whose shaping in the end will only have served to form a work that is lost, their loss is their work. And it will serve, since He cannot be overcome, to make manifest His justice and His power. Whereas the glory of the vessels of mercy —which have not slipped themselves from His hand—is His work ; it is He Who prepared from for glory and in order to make manifest the richness of His glory—a glory after which He seeks, as Saint Thomas Aquinas will put it, not for Himself, but for us, since it consists in freely pouring forth His goodness.

Jeremiah had gone down to the house of the potter. And behold he was working at his wheels. And the vessel he was making was marred, as will happen to the clay in the hand of the potter ; and he made another vessel, as it seemed good in the eyes of the potter to make it [cf. Jer. xviii. 3-4].

It is this image that Paul recalled. When he speaks of the " vessels of wrath " " made for destruction " (not that they were shaped with the intention of being destroyed—the potter would like them all to come perfect—but because in fact they will reach only destruction) he seems to be thinking at once of the historical mystery of peoples and, as though across this perspective, of the eternal mystery of souls. When it comes to peoples, those whom the disfavours of nature and of history prepare for a great ruin carry with them a destiny of misfortune. When it comes to souls and their eternal fate, there is in them no destiny of misfortune. But there are vessels which are *marred*, as will happen to the clay in the hands of the potter, and that, through their free initiative failing, since we are here dealing with intelligent vessels. So likewise Paul says that God suffers with great patience the vessels of wrath. And does he not in the same Epistle recall the words of Isaiah : " All the day long I have stretched out my hands to a people who disobey and contradict " ? And so if the final end to which come rebel souls through their fault is perdition, the initial cause of their loss does not trace back to the will of God, but to themselves. But the punishment of those who have been thus obstinate in evil is willed by God ; and it is by this chastisement of evil, of which evil the initiative comes from the free creature—not by a predestination to evil which it would be blasphemous to attribute to God—that God makes manifest His justice and His power.

What then are we to say ? Is there injustice in God ? Heaven forbid ! For to Moses he saith, "I shall have mercy on whomsoever I shall have mercy, and I shall have pity on whomsoever I shall have pity." [1] So, then it is not a question of man being willing, or running the race, but of the mercy of God. For the scripture saith to Pharaoh, "For this very purpose I have raised thee up, that I may show in thee my power, and that my name may be proclaimed the whole world over." [2] So, then, he hath mercy on whom he will, and whom he will he "hardeneth." [3]

Thou wilt say to me therefore, "Why, then, doth he still find fault ? For who resisteth his will ?" Nay, rather, O man, who art thou, that dost answer back to God ? Shall the thing moulded say to him who moulded it, "Why hast thou made me thus ?" Or hath not the potter power over the clay, so as to make out of the same lump one vessel unto honour, and another unto dishonour ? And what if God, wishing to show his wrath and to make known his power, hath endured with much longsuffering vessels of wrath, fashioned unto destruction ; and in order to make known the riches of his glory upon vessels of mercy, which he hath prepared beforehand unto glory—even ourselves, whom he hath called, not only from among the Jews, but from among the gentiles also ?

Even so he saith in Hosea, "I shall call that my people which was not my people,

and her beloved who was not beloved ;

And it shall be, that in the place where it was said to them, Ye are not my people,

there they shall be called sons of the living God. [4]

And Isaiah doth cry out touching Israel :

"Though the number of the children of Israel be as the sand of the sea, only a remnant shall be saved. For the Lord will execute his word upon the earth, fully and without delay."

---

[1] Exod. xxxiii. 19.   [2] Exod. ix. 16.
[3] Exod. vii. 3.   [4] Hos. ii. 23 ; i. 10 (ii. 1).

It is as Isaiah foretold :

" Unless the Lord of hosts had left us a seed, we should have become
    as Sodom,
and we should have been made like unto Gomorrah." [1] [Rom. ix.
14–29.]

Who is it setteth thee apart from another ? Nay what hast thou
which thou hast not received ? [1 Cor. iv. 7.]

These words are drawn from a context in which Paul
reproaches the quarrelsome among the Corinthians for their
boastfulness, but theologians apply them, and with justice,
too, to the mystery of salvation, by exceeding their immediate,
material meaning.

It is God who worketh in you both the will and the performance,
to fulfil his good pleasure. [Philip. ii. 13.]

The word of God . . . worketh in you that believe. [1 Thes. ii. 13.]

The gift of God operates in us, and makes us act freely,
toward a life which proceeds from the same divine power
as does Christ's Resurrection, and which blossoms out in the
loving knowledge of the mysteries of God the Saviour.

For this cause I also, hearing of the faith in the Lord Jesus which is
among you, and of your charity to all the saints, cease not giving thanks
for you, making remembrance of you in my prayers, in order that the
God of our Lord Jesus Christ, the Father of glory, may grant you the
Spirit of wisdom and revelation unto the full knowledge of himself,
and enlighten the eyes of your heart to know what is the hope of his
calling, what the treasures of the glory of his inheritance among the
saints, what the surpassing greatness of his power towards us that
believe, displayed in the working of the might of his strength. For
with that same strength he has wrought in Christ, raising him from the
dead, and " seating him at his right hand " [2] in the heavenly places,
above every principality and power and virtue and domination, above
every name that is named not only in this world but also in that which
is to come. And " he hath subjected all things beneath his feet," [3]
and hath given him for supreme head to the Church, which is his
body, the fulness of him who is wholly fulfilled in all. [Ephes. i. 15–23.]

Incorporated in the Saviour, we have our share in the

[1] Isa. x. 21–23 ; i. 9.   [2] Ps. cx. (cix.) 1.   [3] Ps. viii. 6.

mystery of the Ascensions, for " our commonwealth is in the heavens." [Philip. iii. 20.]

Ye also were dead in your transgressions and your sins, wherein sometime ye walked after the fashion of this world, under the prince of the power of the air, the spirit which now worketh in the children of disobedience. In their company we too at one time were all living, in indulgence of the desires of our flesh : we were fulfilling the promptings of the flesh and of our minds and were by nature children of wrath like the rest. But God, who is rich in mercy, by reason of his great love wherewith he hath loved us, even when we were dead in our transgressions, brought us to life with Christ—by grace ye are saved —and raised us up and seated us in Christ Jesus in the heavenly places, to show in the ages to come the surpassing riches of his grace through his kindness to us in Christ Jesus. For by grace ye are saved, through faith ; and that not of yourselves, it is the gift of God ; not as the outcome of works, lest any should boast. For we are his handiwork, created in Christ Jesus for good works, which God hath prepared beforehand that therein we may walk. [Ephes. ii. 1–18.]

We are made fellow-citizens of the saints and the dwellingplace of God.

Therefore ye are no longer strangers and foreigners, but ye are fellow-citizens of the saints and members of the household of God : ye are built upon the foundation of the apostles and prophets. Christ Jesus himself is the corner-stone. In him the whole building is duly fitted together and groweth into a temple holy in the Lord ; in him ye also are being built together into a spiritual dwelling-place of God. [Ephes. ii. 19–22.]

We shall judge the angels :

Know ye not that the saints shall judge the world ? And if the world itself is to be judged by you, are you unworthy to judge the veriest trifles ? Know ye not that we shall judge the angels ? How much more matters of everyday life ? [1 Cor. vi. 2–3.]

Nova Creatura

The New Covenant brings a New Law, which is a law of freedom, and it brings a new thing which matters over all others ; it makes new, man himself. Paul exults in this newness.

If then, any man be in Christ, he is a new creature : the former things have passed away : behold, all things are made new. [2 Cor. v. 17.]

Cleanse out the old leaven that ye may be new dough, free from leaven, as indeed ye are. For our " passover hath been sacrificed," [1] even Christ. Wherefore let us hold festival, not with the old leaven nor with leaven of malice and villainy, but with unleavened bread of sincerity and truth. [1 Cor. 7-8.]

Him that knew not sin, for our sakes God made sin, that in him we might become the justness of God. [2 Cor. v. 21.]

The death of Christ, Who is " made sin for our sakes," is a principle of active death with regard to the seed of sin which is in us, and with regard to the " old man," the " natural man " inclined to evil, and crippled as to good. Christ's resurrection, and His life of glory, which is an eternal life, gives life in us to the new man, who is " able to do all in Him Who strengthens him " [cf. Philip. iv. 13]. To make progress, in co-operation with the gift of God, at once in this death and in this life— such is in its essence the spiritual doctrine—ascetic and mystical —of Saint Paul.

If we have become one with him in likeness of his death, why, then we shall also be in likeness of his resurrection. For this we know, that our old man hath been crucified with him, in order that our sinful body may be brought to naught, and ourselves no longer be slaves to sin. [Rom. vi. 5-6.]

In sooth we have heard tell of him and in him ye have been instructed, as in Jesus is truth, that, as regards your former manner of life, ye are to put off the old man who falleth to corruption through deceitful lures of desire, to be renewed in the spirit of your mind, and to put on the new man, who is created according to God in justness and holiness of truth. [Ephes. iv. 21-24.]

The Freedom of the Perfect

In making man through grace a new creature, God calls him to freedom. This freedom of the perfect is won through the Cross, and given by the Spirit.

[1] Exod. xii. 21.

Nay, ye were called to freedom, brethren ; only let not your freedom be an occasion for the flesh ; rather be ye slaves one of another by charity. For the whole of the Law is fulfilled in one sentence, thus, " Thou shalt love thy neighbour as thyself." [1] But if ye bite and devour one another, take heed lest ye be destroyed by one another.

What I say is this : walk in the spirit, and ye will not fulfil the lust of the flesh. For the flesh lusteth against the spirit, and the spirit against the flesh. These are at enmity one with the other, so that ye do not what ye would. But if ye are led by the spirit ye are not under the Law.

Now the works of the flesh are manifest, of which are fornication, impurity, uncleanness, idolatry, witchcraft, enmity, strife, jealousy, wrath, dissensions, factions, parties, envy, drunkenness, revelling and the like. As to which I warn you, as I have warned you before, that they who do such things shall not inherit the kingdom of God. Whereas the fruit of the spirit is charity, joy, peace, patience, kindness, goodness, faithfulness, gentleness, self-control. Against such there is no law. And they that are of Christ Jesus have crucified their flesh with its passions and desires. If we live in the spirit, by the spirit also let us walk. Let us not become vainglorious, provoking one another, envying one another. [Gal. v. 13-16.]

Ye have not yet resisted unto blood in the struggle with sin ; and yet ye have forgotten the exhortation which appealeth to you as sons :

My son, despise not the correction of the Lord,
　　neither lose courage when thou are reproved by him,
For whom the Lord loveth he correcteth
　　and he scourgeth every son whom he accepteth.[2]

What ye endure is unto correction ; as with sons God dealeth with you. For where is there a son that his father doth not correct ? If ye are without correction, in which all have had a share, ye are bastards and not sons. [Heb. xii. 4-8.]

Brethren, unite in imitating me, and take not of those who walk after the model we have given you. For there are many, of whom I have often spoken to you, and speak to you again with tears, enemies of the cross of Christ : whose end is destruction, whose God is their belly, whose glory is in their shame—their minds being set on things earthly. Whereas our commonwealth is in the heavens, whence we eagerly await as saviour the Lord Jesus Christ, who will transform the body of our lowliness, that it may be one with the body of his glory,

---

[1] Levit. xix. 18.　　　　[2] Prov. iii. 11-12.

by the force of that power whereby he is able to subject all things to himself. [Philip. iii. 17–21.]

The law of trial and self-sacrifice is imposed not only for the mortification of evil desires and to keep us safe from the false freedom which Paul depicts and condemns in these sentences from the Epistle to the Philippians which I have just quoted. This is only the beginning and prerequisite of the Christian life. The law of the cross is also imposed, and above all, because we are the members of a crucified Head. This law shapes us to His life and makes us participate in his redeeming labour.

Heirs of God, and joint-heirs with Christ—if, that is, we suffer with him, that with him we may also be glorified. [Rom. viii. 17.]

With Christ I am nailed to the cross : it is no longer I that live, but Christ that liveth in me. [Gal. ii. 20.]

I bear the markings of Jesus in my body. [Gal. vi. 17.]

I make up in my flesh what is lacking to the sufferings of Christ. [Colos. i. 24.]

Nay, all that will to live piously in Christ Jesus shall be persecuted. [2 Tim. iii. 12.]

It is freely and by love, and as to a treasure willingly chosen, that the saints cleave to the sufferings of the Saviour, or rather abandon themselves to the Saviour Who associates them with His Sufferings. Thus the freedom of the perfect is won by the Cross, because we are of one shape with Christ [Philip. iii. 10 ; 21] and called to enter into his work.

And this freedom is given by the Spirit, for it is the Spirit which works in us—in the Christ in Whom we are incorporate —that adoption as sons.

So, then, brethren, we are debtors, not to the flesh, that we should live according to the flesh—for if ye live according to the flesh, ye shall surely die ; but if by the spirit ye do to death the practices of the body, ye shall live. For as many as are led by the Spirit of God, these are the sons of God. For ye have not received the spirit of slavery, to be once more in fear, but ye have received the spirit of adoption, whereby we cry, " Abba ! Father ! " The Spirit himself beareth witness

with our spirit that we are the children of God. And if children,
heirs also : heirs of God, and joint-heirs with Christ—if, that
is, we suffer with him, that with him we may also be glorified.
[Rom. viii. 12-17.]

Now the Lord is the Spirit ; and where the Spirit of the Lord is,
there is freedom. But we all with faces unveiled, reflecting as in a
mirror the glory of the Lord, are transformed into his very image
from glory to glory, as through the Lord the Spirit. [2 Cor. iii. 17-18.]

This doctrine of Saint Paul on liberty is an eternal beacon
for mankind. Saint Thomas Aquinas has developed it in most
profound fashion in Book IV of the *Summa contra Gentiles* :

" We must observe, that the sons of God are led by the Holy
Spirit, not as though they were slaves, but as being free. For,
since to be free is to be cause of one's own actions, we are
said to do freely what we do of ourselves. Now this is what
we do willingly : and what we do unwillingly, we do not
freely but under compulsion. This compulsion may be
absolute, when the cause is wholly extraneous, and the patient
contributes nothing to the action, for instance, when a man is
compelled to move by force : or it may be partly voluntary,
as when a man is willing to do or suffer that which is less
opposed to his will, in order to avoid that which is more
opposed thereto. Now, the Holy Spirit inclines us to act, in
such a way as to make us act willingly, inasmuch as He causes
us to be lovers of God. Hence the sons of God are led by the
Holy Spirit to act freely and for love, not slavishly and for
fear : wherefore the Apostle says [Rom. viii. 15] : *You have
not received the spirit of bondage again in fear ; but you have
received the spirit of adoption of sons.*

" Now the will is by its essence directed to that which
is truly good ; so that when, either through passion or through
an evil habit or disposition, a man turns away from what is
truly good, he acts slavishly, in so far as he is led by something
extraneous, if we consider the natural direction of the will ;
and if we consider the act of the will as inclined here and now
towards an apparent good, he acts freely when he follows
the passion or evil habit, but he acts slavishly if, while his will
remains the same, he refrains from what he desires through

fear of the law which forbids the fulfilment of his desire. Accordingly, when the Holy Spirit, by love inclines the will to the true good to which it is naturally directed, He removes both the servitude whereby a man, the slave of passion and sin, acts against the order of the will, and the servitude whereby a man acts against inclination of his will, and in obedience to the law, as the slave and not the friend of the law. Where the Apostle says [2 Cor. iii. 17] : *Where the Spirit of the Lord is, there is liberty*, and [Gal. v. 18] : *If you are led by the Spirit you are not under the law*." [1]

The Life of the New Man

If then ye have risen with Christ, seek the things that are above, where Christ is " seated on the right hand of God " : mind the things that are above, not the things that are on earth. For ye have died, and your life is hidden with Christ in God : when Christ, our life, shall appear, then also shall we appear with him in glory.

Put to death then, your members that are on earth, even impurity, uncleanness, lust, evil desire, and cupidity (the which is a worship of idols), by reason of which things cometh the anger of God. In such practices ye also did sometimes walk, when ye lived therein. But now do ye also put them all away—anger, indignation, malice, slander, foul-mouthed utterances. Lie not to one another. Strip off the old man with his practices, and put on the new, that is being renewed to fuller knowledge " after the image of his Creator." [2] Herein, there is not gentile and Jew, circumcision and uncircumcision, barbarian, Scythian, slave, freemen, but Christ is all and in all.

Put ye on then, as God's elect, holy and well-beloved, hearts of compassion, kindness, humility, meekness, long-suffering. Bear ye with one another, pardon one another, if one against another have cause of complaint : as the Lord hath pardoned you, so do ye. But over all these put on charity, the bone, that is, of perfection. And in your hearts let the peace of Christ stand supreme, whereunto also ye are called as members of one body ; and be grateful. Let the word of Christ dwell in you richly, so that with all wisdom ye teach and admonish one another, and in psalms, hymns, and spiritual canticles sing in your hearts to God by his grace. And whatsoever ye do in

---

[1] Saint Thomas Aquinas, *Summa contra Gentiles*, iv. 22.
[2] Gen. i. 27.

word or in work, do all in the name of the Lord Jesus, giving thanks to God the Father through him. [Colos. iii. 1-17.]

Whether therefore you eat or drink or do aught besides, do all for the glory of God. [1 Cor. x. 31.]

Piety is profitable for all things, possessing promise of life both here and hereafter. [1 Tim. iv. 8.] ["The whole sum of the Christian discipline consists in mercy and in piety," says the Ambrosian Gloss in connection with this text.]

We exhort ye, brethren, admonish the disorderly, encourage the faint-hearted, support the weak, show patience towards all. See that none return any one evil for evil, but always seek after good both towards one another and towards all.

> Rejoice always,
> Pray without ceasing,
> In everything give thanks ;
> For this is God's will towards you in Christ Jesus.
> Quench not the spirit,
> Spurn not prophesyings ;
> But test all things,
> Hold fast the good,
> Keep yourselves from every form of evil. [1 Thes. v. 14-22.]

Rejoice in the Lord always ; again will I say, rejoice. Let your forbearance be known to all men ; the Lord is nigh. Have no anxieties, but in every circumstance, by prayer and petition joined with thanksgiving, let your requests be made known to God. And the peace of God, which surpasseth all understanding, will guard your hearts and your minds in Christ Jesus.

For the rest, brethren, all that is true, all that is seemly, all that is just, all that is pure, all that is lovable, all that is winning—whatever is virtuous or praiseworthy—let such things fill your thoughts. What ye have learnt and received and heard and seen in me, put that into practice ; and the God of peace shall be with you. [Philip. iv. 4-9.]

Wherefore put away lying and "speak truth, every man with his neighbour," [1] because we are members of one another. "Be ye angry and sin not" ; [2] let not the sun go down upon your anger, and give no place to the devil. Let him that used to thieve thieve no more, but rather labour, working with his own hands at what is good that he may have whereof to impart to him that is in need. Let no tainted

---

[1] Zech. viii. 16.   [2] Ps. iv. 4.

speech issue forth from your mouth, but only what may prove helpful for the occasion and do good to the hearers. And grieve not the Holy Spirit of God, whereby ye have been sealed against the day of redemption. Let all bitterness and wrath and anger and clamour and abusive language be removed from you, and all malice ; be kind to one another, and compassionate, freely pardoning one another, as also God in Christ hath freely pardoned you. Be ye, then, imitators of God, as well-beloved children, and walk in love, as Christ also hath loved you and delivered himself up for us, an offering and sacrifice of sweet savour to God.

But as for impurity and all uncleanness or cupidity, let it not so much as be named amongst you,[1] as becometh saints, no, nor filthiness, and foolish talk, or scurrility, which are not fitting ; but rather giving of thanks. For this know ye and understand, that no impure or unclean or covetous (that is, idolatrous) person hath any inheritance in the kingdom of Christ and God. Let no man deceive you with futile words ; for because of these things cometh the anger of God upon the children of disobedience. Do not then throw in your lot with them : for though ye were sometime darkness, ye are now light in the Lord. Walk as children of light—for the fruit of the light is in all goodness and justness and truth—and find out what is well-pleasing to the Lord. Have no fellowship with the unfruitful works of darkness, but rather expose them. For the things done by such men in secret it is shameful even to speak of ; but all things are exposed and made manifest by the light. For all that is made manifest is light. Wherefore it is said,

> Awake, thou that sleepest,
> And arise from the dead,
> And Christ shall enlighten thee.[2]

Look therefore carefully how ye walk, not as unwise, but as wise, ransoming the time, because the days are evil. Therefore be not foolish, but understand what is the will of the Lord. And be not drunken with wine, wherein is riotousness, but be ye filled with the Spirit, speaking one to another in psalms and hymns and spiritual songs, singing and making melody with your heart to the Lord, giving thanks always for all things in the name of our Lord Jesus Christ

---

[1] *Nec nominatur in vobis.* The meaning of this much-quoted formula is not : " Let the name of these things never be uttered." (Saint Paul himself often speaks of them, and most openly), but " May these things remain so far from your hearts that their very names do not enter your everyday conversations ; may it never even be a matter of discussion whether such things exist among you."

[2] Apparently a quotation from an early Christian hymn.

to God the Father, being subject one to another in the fear of Christ. [Ephes. iv. 25 ; v. 21.]

For the rest, be strong in the Lord and in the might of his power. Put ye on the full armour of God that ye may be able to stand against the wiles of the devil. For our wrestling is not against flesh and blood, but against the principalities, against the powers, against the world-rulers of this darkness, against the spirits of wickedness in regions above. Wherefore take ye up the full armour of God, that ye may be able to resist in the evil day, to do your whole duty and to stand your ground. Stand, then, " with your loins girt in truth," and " having on the breast-plate of justness," and with " your feet " shod " in readiness to carry the gospel of peace," taking up withal the shield of faith, wherewith ye shall be able to quench all the fiery darts of the evil one. And take " the helmet of salvation " and " the sword of the spirit," which is " the word of God." [1]

With all prayer and supplication pray at every season in the spirit ; on that be intent, ever persevering in supplication for all the saints, —and on my behalf also, that such utterance may be given me, when my mouth is opened, that I may fearlessly make known the mystery of the gospel, for the which I am an ambassador in chains, and that I may speak fearlessly thereof, as I ought to speak. [Ephes. vi. 10-20.]

The life of the new man is a thirst to see God, and to be with Jesus.

For we know that if the tent that is our earthly home be destroyed, we have from God a building, a home not made by hands, eternal in the heavens. Yet, in this present abode we groan, yearning to be clothed over with that dwelling-place that is from heaven—if indeed we shall be found clothed at all, and not naked. For we who are in this tent groan under our burden, because we would fain not be unclothed, but rather clothed over, that what is mortal may be swallowed up by life. And he that hath wrought us unto this every end is God, who also hath given us the earnest of his Spirit.

Ever full of courage, then, and knowing that while we are at home in the body we are exiled from the Lord—for we walk by faith, not by sight—yea, we have the courage even to prefer to be exiled from the body and to be at home with the Lord. [2 Cor. v. 1-8.]

I long to dissolve and to be with Christ. [Philip. i. 23.]

---

[1] Cf. Isa. xi. 5

And this thirst begins already to be quenched here below, through the contemplation which proceeds from the union of love with God, in faith, for those who "have come to know God, or rather have come to be known by God" [Gal. iv. 9]. The Spirit of God alone can give it.

For the Spirit exploreth all things, even the depths of God. For who among you knoweth what passeth in man save the spirit of man within him ? Even do the things of God none hath come to know save the Spirit of God. [I Cor. ii. 10–11.]

The Spirit is word, because it gives life to the heart and makes it abound in words—*sermone ditans guttura*—and because it makes descend upon us, into the very substance of our being, everything that Christ has told us. Paul is speaking of the Spirit when he says :

Living is the word of God, and energizing, and keener than any two-edged sword, and penetrating even to the division of soul and spirit, of joints and marrow, and a judge of the thoughts and opinions of the heart. And no creature is hidden before him : everything is revealed and laid bare before the eyes of him to whom we must give reckoning. [Heb. iv. 12–13.]

Thus digging into and stripping our substance, in those mystical purifications of which Saint John of the Cross will later speak, the Spirit of God Himself prepares us for union with our God, Who "is a devouring fire" [Heb. xii. 19]. It is the Spirit who prays in us "with unutterable groanings" [Rom. viii. 26], and who spiritually transforms us in God, in the union of love : "He that cleaveth to the Lord is one spirit with him" [I Cor. vi. 17] ; "two natures in a single spirit and love," as will say Saint John of the Cross. And thereupon man—the new man, the just one who lives of the faith—arrives at the place where there is no further path, at the supreme wisdom ; and free with the freedom of the perfect, truly enters into the depths of God.

For this cause, then, I bend my knees to the Father, from whom all fatherhood in heaven and on earth is named, that he grant you according to the riches of his glory to be strengthened powerfully through his Spirit in the inward man—that Christ may dwell in your hearts through faith, so that rooted and founded in charity, ye may be able to comprehend with all the saints what is the breadth and length and height and depth—to know the charity of Christ that surpasseth knowledge, that ye may be filled unto all the fulness of God.

Now to him that is able to accomplish far beyond all that we ask or understand, through his power that is at work in us—to him be glory in the Church and in Christ Jesus unto all generations, world without end, Amen.   [Ephes. iii. 14-21.]